Dear michell.
Thanks for
your love, comp...
is something !
I feel blessed.
"Life is a blast, it gives us
exactly what we need"

The Secrets of the Rainmaker
Success without Stress

Chin-Ning Chu

Look after yourself.

Love
Vini   ma 99'

xox
ooo

First published in Australia 1997

National Library of Australia Cataloguing-in-Publication entry

Chu, Chin-Ning
Secrets of the Rainmaker/Chin-Ning Chu
ISBN 1 876066 024
   1. Success in business. 2. Success in life. 3. Motivation 4. Leadership
   5. Business philosophy. 6. Inspiration I. Title.

Stealth books are available at special discounts for bulk purchases for sales promotions, premiums, fund-raising or educational use. For details contact:

Special Sales Director
Stealth Productions
PO Box 769
St Ives NSW 2075
Australia

Editor: Rae Blair
Cover design: Toothpicks Creative, Melbourne, Vic.
Typesetting: Go4it Pty Ltd Vic.
Printed by: Griffin Press, SA.

The Secrets of the RAINMAKER

Success Without Stress

Chin-Ning Chu

Stealth Productions Australia

Other books by Chin-Ning Chu

THE ASIAN MIND GAME

THICK FACE BLACK HEART

What Leaders are saying about "Secrets of the Rainmaker"

In this era of mind boggling change and fierce competition, it is necessary for those at the top as well as those who want to get there to develop and excel in the art of quiet listening—to "be still and know..." Chin-Ning has, through elegant but simple language, provided the keys that will unlock your imprisoned splendor.

Secrets of the Rainmaker enriches our lives in every aspect as we empower ourselves to be more effective and productive in our professional and personal lives.

It's a book which leads you on the path to a place of sanity and serenity in this crazy anxiety-driven world. With heart attacks and stress pushing millions over the edge, Chin-Ning shows you how to become centred in the midst of the storm of life and say, "Peace...be still my soul."

— ***Les Brown***, *"Mr Motivator", Author,*
Television and Radio Host

Congratulations Chin-Ning. Finally, someone brave enough to bring some spirit into business.

— ***John Naisbitt***, *Author of* Megatrends *and* Megatrends Asia

In a chaotic world reeling in fast forward, Chin-Ning—the 21st century change master—slows our heartbeat and inspires our soul-deep yearning for authentic, lasting success. Timeless wisdom combined with timely counsel on winning from within.

— ***Dr Denis Waitley***, *Author of* The Psychology of Winning *and* Seeds of Greatness

In *Secrets of the Rainmaker,* Chin-Ning Chu views work in its proper perspective—placing humanity and spirituality in business where they belong—ahead of mere monetary profitability. This perspective will reward business-owners with the ultimate in profitability—a peaceful heart, compatibility with time and a large bank account. Success with stress is not really success at all, and we should all be grateful to this wonderful book for underscoring that crucial truth.

— ***Jay Conrad Levinson***, *Author of* Guerrilla Marketing

I think *Secrets of the Rainmaker* is a crowning magnum opus. I am transforming as I am reading this book. What a masterpiece. Chin-Ning is the greatest Thinker of our time.

— ***James Andrews***, *Dir. of Marketing, Columbia Records/Sony Music*

We fail to achieve our goals because we are trying too hard to succeed. The secret, as Chin-Ning Chu reveals, is finding that balance point between effort and ease.

— ***Scott DeGarmo***, *Publisher of* SUCCESS *magazine*

To my beloved

I am the plant,
you are the water and the nutrients.
The plant gets the glory and is admired.
Yet, without the water and the nutrients,
there would be no plant.

Contents

About Chin-Ning

Born in Tienjin, China, Chin-Ning fled with her family to Taiwan when she was three. At the age of ten, her primary life ambition was to be a saint. In high school, she became a novice at a Catholic convent until her family decided marriage into a family of wealth and status would be a better career path for her.

In college, while still a full-time student struggling for money, she worked for a time as a television soap opera actress for the single station serving all of Taiwan, and then as a marketing representative for one Taiwanese and two European pharmaceutical companies. Being a natural-born entrepreneur with great sales ability, she caused a back-ordering for three months on a brand of cough syrup she pitched to her doctor clients and hospitals. Her earnings at the time were triple that of her professors.

Upon finishing college, she moved to America and has made the United States her home ever since. Today, she is the Chairperson of the Strategic Learning Institute, the President of Asian Marketing Consultants, Inc., and the most successful American author in Asia, where her books have outsold authors such as Stephen Covey, Tony Robbins, and Tom Peters. Her books, *Thick Face Black Heart* and *The Asian Mind Game*, have reached the top of bestseller lists in Australia, Malaysia, Singapore, Indonesia, Taiwan, and China.

Through books, speeches, seminars and tapes, Chin-Ning has touched millions of lives in over forty countries. She is highly revered among notable policy makers, corporate executives, foreign dignitaries, theologians, professors, and even prison inmates. She has received more than ten thousand letters from around the world in which readers have shared their experiences of dramatic life transformations precipitated by her writings.

Chin-Ning's work is highly praised by the international media, including CNN, *USA Today*, the *Financial Times*, *People's Daily* in China, the Asia editions of *People, Bazaar* and *Vogue*, to name a few. She counts a number of prestigious multinational corporations among her clients, who refer to her as "The Bridge to the Pacific Century" and "The Strategist." During the 1996 Democratic presidential convention, she was honoured as Woman of the Year by the international organization, Women of the World.

A most extraordinary thinker, Chin-Ning presents the warrior philosophy of Asia as the premier vehicle for mastering strategic thinking in the corporate world as well as in daily life. She fuses timeless wisdom and spirituality with practical business tactics for solving life's ever-changing challenges.

Foreword

In his classic book, *The Road Less-Traveled*, M. Scott Peck begins with the declaration, "Let's face it, life is difficult."

In this destined-to-be-classic book, Chin-Ning Chu makes the case for life being easy.

If, after reading the wisdom inscribed on the pages that follow, you still can't grasp the idea that life was meant to be easy, I am certain you will understand the brilliance of *Success without Stress:* what appears simple is profound. What is most profound is so because of its simplicity. What is simple should be easy to embrace.

Chin-Ning Chu, the global strategist and visionary, is a profoundly insightful individual from very humble origins. She has that rarest of gifts...the ability to explain complex, timeless truths in understandable, meaningful metaphors and illustrations.

She is the only person in the world who could have written this book. It is more a painting than an assembly of words. More an awakening within than experiential advice.

Success without Stress addresses the very glue that holds our society together. We have everything going for us, but too little coming together. We seem to have been shoved into a race we didn't choose and whose finish line we can't picture. Most of us have houses, but not the domestic lives we long for. We have photo albums and videotapes of our children, but not the spiritual strength that underpins healthy families. We're extremely busy, sometimes frantically busy, but we don't quite know where we're going. We cope with the urgent, but keep putting off what we sense is truly important. We try to squeeze in lots of fun, sometimes expensive fun, but we're not really happy. Some of us are doing the right things at the wrong time; some are doing the wrong things all the time.

Most of us believed the computer would give us more time for leisure and personal pursuits. Designed as a tool for managing complexity, it also adds complexity, just as new freeways add more traffic. The computer enables us to sort, store, and retrieve material with ever-increasing speed. But the faster that data can be analyzed, the faster decisions are expected and the greater the pressure to reach them.

As we enter a new millennium, we must reexamine and reevaluate the way we think, the way we respond to life's daily challenges in what will be a time of even more astonishing change. Technology, with all its wondrous multi-media graphics, has become the enemy of intimacy.

And in our global village, where communication and transportation have made neighbours of all who live on earth, the closeness of our geography has actually spawned more suspicion, prejudice and animosity toward one another.

In this new era in which knowledge is the new power and where enlightenment and spirituality can become the seeds of harmony and greatness for the human race, we need to break the cycle. We are in the midst of one of the most threatening cultural droughts in history.

Thankfully, Chin-Ning has summoned The Rainmaker.

— Denis Waitley
President of The Waitley Institute, author of 12 non-fiction books, including national bestsellers: Seeds of Greatness *and* Empires of the Mind. *His audio album,* The Psychology of Winning *sold over 10 million sets in 14 languages.*

The Rainmaker

Carl Jung, Sigmund Freud's premier student in the field of psychoanalysis, often spoke of the power of miracles by telling the following story:

There was a village that had been experiencing drought for five consecutive years. Many famous rainmakers had been called, but they had all failed to make rain. In the villagers' last attempt, they called upon a renowned Rainmaker from afar. When he arrived in the village, all he did was set up his tent and disappear inside it for four days. On the fifth day, the rain started to fall and quenched the thirst of the parched earth. The people of the village asked the Rainmaker how he had accomplished such a miracle.

The Rainmaker replied, "I have done nothing."

Astounded at his explanation, the villagers said, "How can that be? After you came, we had rain for four continuous days."

The Rainmaker explained, "When I arrived, the first thing I noticed was that everything in your village was out of harmony with heaven. So I spent four days putting myself into harmony with the Divine. Then the rains came."

TIRED OF CHASING

Life was meant to be easy; as easy as the Rainmaker effortlessly made rain. Somehow, through the chaos of our thoughts chasing after our heart's desires, we have been holding hostage our primal, native ability to have whatever we want to the fullest.

Many people who chanced to cross my path during my travels have confided in me, "I am so tired of struggling and fighting life's battles on every front in an exhausting attempt to get ahead." Even those who achieve the material prosperity for which we all strive are beset by an uneasiness that mars the unfettered enjoyment of the fruits of their labour.

We often spend so much time working that we have little time left for ourselves. Minds get agitated, hearts grow uninspired, and bodies become weary. Everyone seems to be doing more and, despite their best efforts, there is always more to do. The more money that is made, the more that is needed. When we grow wealthy and prosperous, we find that there are always new frontiers waiting to be conquered. The vicious cycle goes on. How much stress can one's nerves endure?

Even for those who bravely keep their thoughts to themselves, it is easy to see in their eyes, their voice, their body language, and every aspect of their being the same story: "I am tired of chasing; yet, I am caught in a no-win, no-way-out situation. If I don't keep moving faster, the people coming up from behind will trample me. If I don't like where I am right now, how will I like it when I'm relegated to the bottom of the social pyramid? I must pick myself up each day and fight another agonizing, vicious battle." So many have fought bravely, with a lack of joy and an absence of fun in their pursuit of this game called 'Success.'

The solution to this crisis seems to dictate that you give up life, become a hermit, retreat from the world, and live in simplicity with nature. For a small handful, this might be a viable solution. However most of us can't just give up on life because we aren't winning. As a great nineteenth-century Asian master said of one attempting to leave the world after he had failed to manifest his life's dreams, "He did not renounce the world; the world renounced him."

Whether you are chasing success, sustaining your hard-won success or preventing failure, it is often all very stressful. As you reach out to force events and outcomes to bend in your favour, you may experience anxiety. When things are not going your way, it's as if your life has a will of its own.

RELEASING FROM EFFORT

To illustrate: all of my life I wanted to be a great singer. I have spent more money on voice lessons than anything else. During the writing of this book, I realized the main reason I was not the singer I wanted to be was that my desire to sing well was so strong that it had caused my mind to hold my voice hostage. When I sang, instead of just letting my voice go and simply singing, my mind would try to help my voice to sing. I recognized that, in fact, my voice always knew, within itself, how to sing. It was my mind that did not know how to sing.

As I released my mind from the effort of trying to sing, my voice was freed instantly. I came to see that the transformation of any aspect of our lives can be accomplished beyond the constraints of time. This awesome power resides like a seed held within us in much the same way that a seed holds within itself, and ultimately releases, its hidden power of life to become a bountiful tree.

What I discovered about why I couldn't sing provided me with the insight that life was meant to be as easy as singing. Somehow, somewhere along the way of our growing up and growing older, we became all twisted up thinking the way to be successful is to put forth a tremendous effort, attempting to bend events to the ways we have envisioned. The result is that life often doesn't submit to our efforts; rather, we bend ourselves out of shape—stressed out and burned out.

Twenty years ago, I owned an executive employment agency. In the first two weeks after I opened shop, I placed three separate 2.5 cm long ads in the *Los Angeles Times* Sunday Edition in search of three executives for three separate multinational companies. In two days, the three 2.5 cm ads brought me three perfect executive candidates and I quickly sealed the deals. Ironically, my three client companies had also placed three separate large display ads in the same Sunday paper, one ad covering more than a quarter page. Yet, the three qualified candidates answered only my small ads. Miracles happen much more often than we are willing to acknowledge.

This miraculous and simple power exists limitlessly within the laws of nature, totally free, waiting only to be induced. If we were able to call upon the miracle-creating power at any moment we desire, wouldn't our life become like a sleek vessel sailing on a soft, breezy ocean? Unfortunately, it is not so easy.

CONCLUSION

What the Rainmaker did was nothing short of creating a miracle. Although miracles are beyond reason and manipulation, you will find that they can be induced by creating an environment within yourself that attracts the elements of synchronicity and hidden coherence. You will come to see all miraculous incidents as the realization of *the law of synchronicity and hidden coherence*. In our everyday life, we normally don't call them miracles because the word 'miracles' sounds too miraculous. When things miraculously turn out in our favour, we try to underplay them; we call them good luck. Yet so much of this 'good luck' is nothing short of miraculous.

Is there a scientific formula to cause the miracle and good luck to happen on command? Our challenge is to discover what constitutes favourable factors that create the results we desire. In other words, if we can increase our odds to generate beneficial results in our lives and work, our success will be achieved effortlessly as the Rainmaker did. These are the objectives that we will explore throughout the scope of this book.

1st Secret:
Create a harmonious inner environment

The Rainmaker sees that the village is out of harmony, so he first puts himself into harmony and then he attracts the rain. The first secret of the Rainmaker is his ability to create a harmonious inner environment absent of overwhelm and uneasiness. By transforming his interior environment into a magnet he draws to him all good things that are in line with the will of Heaven.

Creating a harmonious inner environment is a good idea and a simple principle, however, it is easier said than done. In order for the mind to release the deathlike grip it uses to hold our lives in place, the mind must feel free to let go. However, merely telling the mind to relax and trust in the Universal Magic will not bring it to relaxation, because, for most of us mortals, it is difficult to purge the mind of panic. In this book we will take each of the Rainmaker's secrets and examine them from multiple angles and perspectives.

As you read on, becoming closer to the experience of the Rainmaker's magical state, you will see how the power of synchronicity works—from the telephone ringing just as you think about the caller, to the creating of a miracle-filled, rain-making life and expediting your grandest life objectives. Good things will simply occur spontaneously.

Secret 1.1:
Do less, achieve more

During an interview, my favourite operatic tenor, Luciano Pavarotti, spoke of how difficult it was to be noticed on the already very crowded world stage of superior tenors. The key to his success, he said, was that he learned the secret of singing an entire opera with a totally relaxed voice.

One of the main principles taught in *hatha* yoga, the Indian system of physical postures, is to allow the body to relax into a given yoga stretch instead of pushing the body into the desired posture. When you are anxious to get into the full extension and you coerce your body into position, the body inevitably resists.

When your mind is open and relaxed, working without effort, not attempting to get anywhere, the body opens from inside naturally and allows you to ease into deep and complete stretching. Our attitudes toward success and the obtaining of the symbols of achievement work much the same way.

THE RELATIONSHIP OF ANXIETY AND REGRESSION

When you are pursuing success with anxiety, it takes a tremendous effort to realize a meager result. You are desiring and thinking so much that you are tired even before you start to work. Though your body has performed no task, your mind has been working hard at fighting and resisting your perceived circumstances. Prior to moving a single muscle, the mind has travelled high and low, through glory and defeat. So much energy is expended within the mind before you have had the chance to engage it in the valid pursuit of your goals. The anxiety of wanting has driven you ever further from achieving what you want.

To act, one needs to be driven by the desire for accomplishment. When that drive is misdirected, we become as ineffective as a wound-up mechanical doll, spinning involuntarily. We want to be relaxed, but don't know how to let go of the thousand details that should have been done *yesterday*. When we force ourselves to slow down, we feel guilty.

THE RHYTHM OF EASE AND EFFORT

We think that making an effort is the opposite of being at ease. The paradoxical truth is that effort and ease are not in opposition—they complement each other. Like an Olympic runner, to win a competition you must put forth much effort. Yet, in order to ensure maximum performance, you must strike a balance between the effort of striving and the ease of fluid action. The same holds true for figure-skating. When skaters put forth too much energy, they over-spin and fall. On the other hand, if they don't give their optimal mental and physical effort, they will fall short of their best performance.

The goal to seek in the expending of effort is to have it become effortless. As a ballerina dances on her toes, her beauty and grace show through because of the endless hours of practice she puts in. Earlier in this book, I mentioned that Luciano Pavarotti has trained himself to sing an entire opera with his voice totally relaxed. In order to have this relaxed voice, he had to train every part of his body to handle the exertion that allows his voice to be relaxed. The secret of success that guides the mastery of a world-class singer, runner or dancer stems from the same principles that lead to a superior manager, salesperson or entrepreneur.

THE HARMONY OF COMPROMISE AND STRIVING

Within the dualistic nature of success is the power of compromise and striving. Think of how a river embodies these two natures. It compromises with the geographical terrain, eroding and smoothing the way as it goes, while relentlessly flowing forward, striving to achieve its ultimate purpose of uniting with the ocean. These two natures are always simultaneously in balance.

The river prioritizes its effort: it has no time to stop flowing and focus on destroying a single obstructing rock before pressing onward. Gushing on to the ocean is its first goal, and removing the rock is its second. While achieving its first objective, it never loses sight of its secondary objective.

In this same manner, while you put forth your exertions in striving to accomplish, remain ever diligent with a watchful eye, seeking out the rhythm of ease.

DO LESS, ACHIEVE MORE

Our personal desire to reach the highest, farthest, brightest star is a noble aspiration, but our ability to reach that star is not in direct proportion to the amount of pain or agony we generate in the process. Nor does it happen within the time line that we artificially impose upon ourselves.

Following are the key points that will allow you to achieve more results while doing less:

1. Let your eyes see

A friend once told me about a book that defined a method of how to correct nearsightedness. I asked him to tell me, in a nutshell, what the book said. When he explained the exercises, one concept really struck a chord within me. The theory was: *when one exerts effort by reaching out toward an object with sight and tries very hard to see it, in time this damages the eye's ability to focus naturally. Most people are struggling to see instead of simply letting their eyes see.* This rudimentary statement echoes the hidden law that guides every aspect of successful human interaction.

In the universe, everything is about this balance between energy and ease. Exert too much effort, and you can become a hindrance to your own progress. Whenever you make an effort, you must simultaneously pull back from your exertions and let the situation happen by unfolding naturally.

2. Let the water boil

In order to boil water, you pour it into a kettle and place the kettle over a fire. These actions all involve expending energy. When you close the lid of the kettle, you *let* the water boil. If you become too anxious about the result and keep opening the lid, you hinder the process of heating up the water, and you delay its boiling.

The same kind of process can occur, for instance, when you must make an oral presentation. You should prepare meticulously, but once that is done, the presentation should take place in an atmosphere of total ease which allows it to unfold naturally and assume its own shape and form.

3. Give your willpower a rest

Willpower is a vital element in completing a job. What works against people who have a strong mind and a determined will is that they often make a victim of their bodies and their peace of mind.

Don't only use the energy of your will. You know you have a very strong mind; you can always count on it being there to support your work. Conversely, without a healthy body and a tranquil mind, no work will be performed anyhow.

Build up your body and health so that they will support your work efforts naturally. Sometimes we miss our great goals by not remembering and living by what seems, on the surface, to be profoundly simple.

4. Know what to give up

Focus your resources—know what to give up and what to pursue. I watched the fortunes of a small European publisher who had been scraping by for a long time. Last year, his company published a book that hit the all-time bestseller list. Due to this unexpected success, he had many prestigious authors approach him for publication of their new books.

This publisher wanted to capitalize on his momentum and publish the new books as soon as possible. However, his company did not have the resources to properly publish these unplanned books. In order to accomplish the task, he had to quickly hire more editors and support personnel, most of whom were inexperienced and not up to the Herculean job. The publisher drove all of his employees into a state of physical and emotional fatigue, with the inevitable result that the work was not carefully supervised.

The books were rushed onto the market, and the quality was an embarrassment to both the publisher and the authors. Furthermore, to fund his expansion, the publisher had exhausted the cash flow created from the original hit book. This led to his premier author suing him for withholding royalty payments. He had bitten off more than he could swallow and ended up with no subsequent hit books and a large financial loss.

Like this publisher, many of us go through a hard learning curve. We are sometimes motivated by fear and greed and become willing to bend our standards 'just a little.' Yet, as we look back, 'sure-fire' deals rarely bring satisfactory results.

5. Stop chasing good opportunities

When we have lived long enough, watched ourselves carefully enough, and learned from our mistakes, eventually we stop panicking and chasing after every 'good' opportunity.

A while ago, I received a phone call from a businessman in Singapore. He asked me to go to Beijing to discuss an upcoming international technology transfer conference. He had arranged for me to meet with Li Peng, the Premier of China at the time, and Zhu Rong Ji, the mastermind of modern Chinese economic development and the present premier.

The Singaporean told me that he had been promoting me to these top Chinese officials and that I would be the ideal person to headline at this event. The conflict was that I had already made a commitment to appear at the Southern Book Fair in Nashville, Tennessee. The Southern Book Fair was not a big event on a national scale, and I was not the only author scheduled to appear there. I could have cancelled the appearance, since it had been set up six months in advance, but I did not feel that would be right. I chose to pass on meeting the top officials in China.

My decision not to meet Li Peng was not based only on the fact that the book fair's brochure had been printed with my name on it, or that my publisher would have been disappointed by my absence. My decision was based on my knowledge that if I am destined to be a great name in my field of discipline, it will happen no matter what I do. Meeting Li Peng will not make it happen. He receives thousands of 'faceless' guests every year—I would be just another body parading before him. One meeting would not give me the privilege of picking up a phone and calling him for a favour. However, I would have definitely generated stress and chaos for myself and others by changing my committed schedule.

21

After many years of trying too hard, now I approach my own destiny calmly instead of frantically chasing every 'good opportunity.' If the angel of good fortune is running hard to chase me, I must slow down enough to let her catch up.

6. Stop running

There are some who may work harder than others, but when the angel of good fortune comes to visit, she seems to pass over them. They are so busy trying to network; they attend every association meeting; they become a permanent fixture at all the parties and meeting halls.

Mr Lam is such a person. He spent twenty years living and working in America. Two years ago, his father passed away and left him with a 'not so healthy' family business. Mr Lam moved his family back to Hong Kong and began his struggle with this business, which seemed to have a mind of its own and a distinct lack of will to live.

Because Mr Lam had been away from Hong Kong for a long time, he felt that he needed to rebuild his connections. He started by attending every political and business function. He spent a minimum of six out of every seven evenings performing his self-imposed professional obligations of social drinking, eating, and networking.

Every event coordinator who needed a warm body knew he could count on Mr Lam. After all of these efforts, Mr Lam's business was still in a half-dead state with no significant improvement. As I looked at him, I thought to myself that he had acted like a desperate chicken with his head cut off, moving without direction.

Since the 80/20 rule states that "eighty percent of one's business income will be derived from twenty percent of one's clients," Mr Lam's time and energy would have been spent much more productively if he had simply relaxed at home or read a good book. Then, when he felt nurtured, with his productivity up, his creativity at a new high, and his spirit rejuvenated, he could have made contact with potential clients he had carefully selected and cultivated. He would then have possessed a strong, calm spirit that could lead him much more effectively toward his desired business ends.

7. Let the angel of good fortune catch up

Richard is a self-employed entrepreneur. He is energetic, aggressive, and smart. However, for a long time, he was not very successful. It was not because he hadn't tried, but rather because he tried too hard and too much. Those projects that he suspected had a handsome monetary reward, he pursued with the intensity of a bulldog grasping a bone. Richard suffo- cated the deals to death.

When he went on a sales call, he didn't stop selling even after the buyer had decided to buy. The buyer may have felt complete with Richard's presentation, but Richard did not experience that completion. It had been too easy for him, so he felt he had to say more. After that, he still felt incomplete and would say just a little more—until he annoyed the buyer, talked himself out of the deal, and was shown the door.

Richard would call his business partners at all hours of the day or night when he felt like taking care of business. The problem was he always felt like taking care of business. His business partners' wives became furious with Richard's all- hour telephone air raids.

I chanced to run into Richard a few months ago. When he told me of his recent successes, I asked him what had changed in his life. He replied, "I have learned to control my urge to overdo and sabotage myself. I have stopped frantically running after success. I slowed down my pace and let the angel of good fortune catch up with me."

8. Success is the living breath of your immortality

Like Richard, many of us are aimlessly moving forward, frantically chasing after elusive success, unaware that we have passed our destination. Knowing how to exist in harmony with the universal forces and finding that balance point between effort and ease is the key to opening the gate to miracles —the creation of synchronistic energy. That opening allows for divine intervention to enter our lives and begin a partnership with us.

For those of you who are fortunate enough to discover early the unfolding pattern of your life, you will come to know the eternal truth that only those who partake of the success within their souls know the success that runs throughout nature. Whosoever lacks this inner success feels also a lack of it in the world. How can one know what success is like if one has never tasted it? However, one who has inner success can abide in this state even in the midst of outer discord. Success is ultimately the living breath of God's immortality within you. It is never apart from you, whatever your temporary circumstance.

9. Know the magnetic power of contentment

The word *contentment* often implies desirelessness and seems to contradict the mental state needed for aspiring to success. When you are seeking the consummation of a given goal or object, you are presumably in a state of longing or incompleteness—a state of non-contentment.

However, when you employ the power of contentment to realize a goal, you are not inactive. Rather, by embracing contentment while doing your job, you remain focused on reaching that brightest star in your personal constellation. All actions that are performed in contentment become charged with the force of progress and growth, and the joy of self-discovery.

When you work in contentment, each day will bring with it a new perspective on how to approach your projects. When you are open, you will experience the joy of performing your work 'in the moment.' The worker and the joy of working create a dynamic synergy that, over the span of time, can bring results beyond your wildest expectations. How can one achieve this attitude of contentment? The way is to be contented even when you are not content.

There lived an old man in his eighties who had been miserable and pessimistic all his life. Nothing ever pleased him. Then one day, out of nowhere, he completely changed. He became optimistic, happy, and possessed of a good and kind nature. The people of his village asked him, "What made you change so suddenly?"

The old man replied: "All of my life I have been upset because I wanted to have a contented mind, but I got nothing for my efforts. Finally, I got so disgusted, I decided to be contented without having a contented mind."

CONCLUSION

The angel of success is a tough mistress. She wants you to pursue her, and yet she will surely elude you if you strive too hard. In order to capture her, you need to pursue her with your best effort while giving her the space to come to you. The motivational force that propels you to pursue success is rooted in dissatisfaction. In order for you to experience any degree of success, you need to incorporate an atmosphere of ease.

When the Rainmaker first arrived in the village the drought was severe and disastrous. In order to bring about the desired result, he released his mind's inner desire to 'fix' the condition. He glided into meditation. By embracing ease, he brought the state of harmony unto himself, and thus it over-flowed into the whole village. By doing less, the Rainmaker achieved more.

Such is the power of ease.

SUMMARY

- We think that making an effort is the opposite of being at ease. The paradoxical truth is that effort and ease are not in opposition—they complement each other.

- The goal to seek when expending effort is to have it become effortless.

- All actions that are performed in contentment become charged with the force of progress and growth, and the joy of self-discovery.

- When you work in contentment, each day will bring with it a new perspective on how to approach your projects. When you are open, you will experience the joy of performing your work 'in the moment.'

- The worker and the joy of working create a dynamic synergy that, over the span of time, can bring results beyond your wildest expectations.

- How can one achieve this attitude of contentment? The way is to be contented even when you are not content.

- The angel of success is a tough mistress. In order to capture her, you need to pursue her with your best effort while giving her the space to come to you.

- The motivational force that propels you to pursue success is rooted in dissatisfaction. In order to experience any degree of success, you need to incorporate an atmosphere of contentment. Such is the paradoxical nature of success.

- Do less, achieve more
    1. Let your eyes see.
    2. Let the water boil.
    3. Give your willpower a rest.
    4. Know what to give up.
    5. Stop chasing good opportunities.
    6. Stop running.
    7. Let the angel of good fortune catch up.
    8. Success is the living breath of your immortality.
    9. Know the magnetic power of contentment.

Secret 1.2:

When you are willing to not survive, you will thrive

Just imagine if our Rainmaker had thought to himself when he entered the village, "I better do a good job making rain. If I don't cause the rain to fall, the villagers will be very upset with me. They will demand their money back. They will tell other villages that I am a lousy rainmaker, that I am a fake. Then, my reputation will be ruined. My business will go down the tubes; my creditors will come after me. I may be forced to declare bankruptcy. I will lose face and bring shame to my family. My wife will divorce me. She will take my kids, my house, my savings. I'm doomed. Oh, my God, please let it rain for me; if you don't, I'll have to kill myself. No, I don't really have the guts to kill myself. But, I don't have the guts to live either...O God, why don't you send a little rain?... you are so stingy...A little rain won't hurt you ...God damn it, rain! I am sorry, I shouldn't curse the Almighty. I take it back. Forgive my sins. But...why can't you just send a little rain? If you let it rain this time, I will donate ten percent of my total income every year to your church. Ok, ok, twenty five percent...is that gross or net? Please I beg of you..." Of course this would not be the way to bring harmony to himself or to the villagers.

Fear of not being able to survive paralyzes us from engaging with life; it holds us back from everything we attempt to accomplish. Humans are perpetual self-learning entities. Everything we do in life, small or large, is motivated by our will to survive. We mentally record events and behaviours that support our survival. Then we repeat that behaviour throughout our life, even if that behaviour is destructive.

BE WILLING NOT TO SURVIVE

Jimmy is a young black professional who opened a computer graphic consulting business with his partner, Gregory. Both partners needed to do the odd jobs around the office such as addressing shipping labels, taping boxes for shipping, organizing files and disks, dropping the mail at the post office. Jimmy's error rate at performing these simple jobs was around sixty percent; tasks that most ten-year-olds could accomplish at 95% accuracy. His excuse was, "I am not good at mundane tasks." Yet these mundane tasks were not brain surgery or rocket science that certain people just couldn't master due to lack of ability.

His error rate was so grossly high that Gregory always had to salvage his mistakes. Once Jimmy taped the top of a shipping box without taping the bottom. When the box arrived at the customer's site, there was nothing in the box. He was a walking disaster. Whenever he touched something, chaos ensued and damage control followed. Jimmy's lack of respect for doing the 'mundane' work caused many arguments between the two partners. They could not afford to hire an outside helper to do the jobs that Jimmy was supposed to be able to handle. Out of desperation, Gregory insisted Jimmy participate in a self-help workshop. During the workshop, the truth flashed to Jimmy.

In Jimmy's mind, he felt he was a 'slave' when doing mundane work. In order to resist being a slave, he learned from very young to screw up every mundane task ever assigned to him. In this way, no one would ever hire him as a potential 'labour' worker. The only problem was that he became so convinced that he had to screw up the simple tasks to enhance his opportunity for personal survival that he ended up sabotaging himself and his partner's business.

Liz is a business equipment salesperson. She figured the way to make herself very important to her sales manager, so that her manager couldn't do without her, was to withhold information from her boss. Whenever her boss tried to obtain information from her on a particular customer, it was like pulling teeth. She always told as little as possible. Eventually her boss became tired of her manipulation and told her, "As long you think you need to survive by manipulating and withholding information from me, you'll be out the door very quickly. You must serve me the way I want to be served, not the way your mind has calculated how to enhance its chance for personal survival. Only when you are willing to not survive, you will thrive."

BE WILLING TO FACE THE WORST CONSEQUENCES

In order to create a harmonious inner environment, you need to be willing to not survive. However, there is no way that you will be willing to not survive. After all, only for the purpose of survival do you strive for success. To put this issue to rest you need to deal with the core matter of life and death. If we are clear about life and death then survival takes care of itself. The fear of not surviving is, of course, rooted in the fear of death.

As long as you are clinging to life at all costs, there is no peace and harmony within. The more you fear not surviving, the tighter you cling to ill-calculated survival strategies until you squeeze the very life out of everything you do. Eventually, simple tasks such as closing a sale or making a presentation are blown out of proportion in your mind into life-or-death situations and you shut out opportunity and vitality from your life.

The thirteenth century Hindu philosopher, Shankaracharya, said, "Even the greatest warrior, when standing in the midst of the battlefield, sweats with fear. However, while his body is fearful and his mind is fearful, his spirit is fearless." Even though I thought I understood these words, not until writing this chapter did I really understand the full scope of the meaning contained therein.

I have never been in the midst of a battle with bombs exploding over my head and bullets dancing all around me, but when I watch a war film I often ask myself the question, "What would I do if I were in that battle?" I would probably be busy looking for the deepest hole in which to hide. Yes, that would be my first instinct. Nonetheless, when I knew there was no use hiding, I would probably grasp onto the spirit of death and do my duty.

As soon as I switch my mind from the fear of being harmed to embracing the spirit of death, immediately the fear flees and death becomes my protector. In this state, I feel so much more alive and powerful.

In the trials of your life, instead of acting gutless, embrace the possibility of not surviving and be willing to face the worst of consequences. You will find there a sudden burst of blissful courage that is rooted in your willingness to not survive. When you see death as the sublime manifestation of the Creator, the identical twin to birth, then death is not so horrible. When you are truly willing to face death, its spirit will protect you from the fear of being harmed.

DEATH WILL PROTECT YOU FROM HARM

My assistant, Tim, told me of an incident that occurred to him one night after a speaking engagement in Washington, D.C. Walking back to his hotel, he took a route which transversed a very progressive neighbourhood located on the fringe of an area known for its riots. As he ambled along, he noticed he was being followed by about a dozen gang members.

The faster he walked, the faster they pursued him. A chase ensued. Tim found himself running deeper into an area of D.C. that was foreign to him. Right on his heels, they were chasing him relentlessly. He thought to himself, "Well, this is it." He began to accept the possibility that tonight would be the night he would die.

As he considered this eventuality, he resolved himself to his fate. In a flash of inspiration, he abruptly stopped running and turned to face the gang. An idea blazed luminously in his mind—if he must die at this moment, his death was not his end. And since his death was not the end, it must at least be the beginning of some new experience. In short, quite possibly, death would not be so bad after all. As the Sufi poet Rumi said, "My death is my wedding with eternity."

Facing the gang members, now gathered in a circle about him, he noticed that there was a thick, invisible energy wall between him and his pursuers. This wall, he realized, had been created by the power of his mind and spirit coming to terms with his imminent 'fate.'

Although the gang wanted to harm him, they seemed powerless to penetrate this invisible, protective psychic wall. The gang felt the fearlessness within Tim. With the intimidation element removed from the space, the thrill of experiencing their power to harm had vanished.

The leader of the gang dropped his menacing stance, stepped forward and, stretching out his hand, said, "What's up, man?" They shook hands and then walked their separate ways. Tim's new friend, death, had defended him.

KNOW HOW TO THRIVE

The principle that Tim applied on the street also works in business. In business, the more fearful you are about your survival, the more mistakes you will tend to make. When you are willing to focus on the duty, risk, exhilaration and the fun of doing it, rather than on the fear of personal survival, you will begin to understand the meaning of thriving.

LIVING WELL, DYING WELL

In comic drawings, death is often portrayed as a black shadow, the grim reaper, a symbol of fear—unholy and evil. This is the myth. What is the reality?

A great saint said, "The purpose of living is to prepare for the moment of death. By preparing for death, one learns how to live well." I mean living well, not just surviving.

One of Confucius' students asked him how to honour the spirits. Confucius replied, "You do not even know how to honour mankind, how can you think of honouring the spirits?" Then the student asked, "May I ask what will happen when I die?" Confucius replied, "When you do not know how to live, how can you ask about how to die?"

If you learn how to live well, then death will take care of itself. Only in living well can one learn how to die. However, life is full of contradiction. In order to live well, one must conquer the fear of living. Befriending death is the quickest way to overcome the fear of dying, which in turn is the source of the fear of living. This is manifested in millions of faces fearing to make business decisions, fearing to take calculated risks, fearing commitment, fearing the making of mistakes, fearing confrontation, fearing heights, fearing water, fearing fear, fearing life. This concept is not derived from a linear logic; it is an experiential truism.

FEARLESSNESS

When a spiritual seeker conquers death during meditation, he then enters into a state of fearlessness for the rest of his earthly life. As St Paul said, "In Christ, I die daily." What he meant was that, through the teachings of Christ, he had learned the secret of overcoming death and was consequently without any trace of the fear of death. Thus, one who knows the mystery of death has no fear of living.

DEATH WILL COME TO YOUR RESCUE

When you are clinging to survival, you find no peace or harmony in your life. No fun in your job. Imagine that God comes to you and tells you that you are going to die one year from now. God says: "For the next year, you will enjoy good health, and your death will be painless. Your only job now is to live a harmonious life. However, you must work. You cannot go out, charge up your credit cards, and blow your savings accounts."

Make a list of what your life would be like for the next year. Then make another list of what your life would be like if you carried on your business as usual. Compare the two lists. Ask yourself the question, what makes the two lists so different? The answer probably has something to do with fear. Due to your fear of suffering the consequences of doing the wrong thing, making the wrong decisions, you jeopardize your personal and career survival. So you handle your business and life with 'business as usual.'

If you knew you were going to die soon, you would not be so concerned about survival. Even if you made mistakes, the consequences would not be so awful, because death would come to your rescue. However, whether it be one year, three years, or thirty years, death will always come to your rescue. What is there to fear? The worst that can happen is death, and when you truly know what death is, that is not such a bad option.

For the people who have encountered death and have returned to tell their stories, the one thing they all have in common is that they no longer operate their life timidly. They open themselves up for challenges. They receive life as an adventure instead of a torturous ordeal. Suddenly, their business and personal lives are full of choice and freedom. You often hear stories about people who, having encountered a death experience, state that their life, their business, their relationships, everything became better.

As Jack London said, "The proper function of man is to live, not to exist." The only reason we find ourselves existing instead of living life is that we are blocked by fear of not surviving. When we befriend death, it protects us from the inherent harm of the world. This creates tremendous freedom and peace inside.

CONTEMPLATING DEATH CREATES HARMONY

The following is a partial list of benefits that lead to the inner harmony I have seen manifest unfailingly when one spends time contemplating the state of death. I am sure you will be able to add more to this list.

1. It keeps us focused on what is truly important in our daily lives.

2. It puts problems in their proper perspective so they seem less troublesome.

3. It decreases our stress level.

4. It focuses the heart on love. We come to know that the purpose of living is to know love.

5. It helps us to calm our minds.

6. It intensifies our connectedness with our Creator.

7. It focuses us to act with more discrimination when the temptations of greed and questionable opportunities present themselves.

8. It cultivates the profound state of detachment from loss and gain. It gives us equal vision about temporary success and failure.

9. It fortifies within us the freedom and courage to do what we are supposed to do—not what is expedient and comfortable.

10. It crystallizes within us the conviction that the purpose of life is to prepare us for the moment of death; that we are accountable and everything we do matters.

11. It gives us fearlessness, for the source of all fear is rooted in the fear of death.

12. Most of all, it will break our survival mode so that we can enjoy and thrive in our life and career.

O DEATH, WHERE IS THY STING?

As I mentioned before, death is often portrayed as a black shadow, the symbol of all things evil and unholy. No wonder people are afraid of death. I would like to submit a view to the contrary: death is the sunshine of new possibilities, a celebration of consummation with eternity. I remember once hearing these words of wisdom: "Men laugh with joy when a child is born, while the child cries alone in grief. Men weep in sorrow when their loved ones die, while the dead one rejoices alone." The power of death not only serves those who have gone before us, it is also there to serve the living who take the requisite time to contemplate the lessons contained in its mystery.

As I have stated, before you can be truly free to live, you must be free to confront your deepest fears that hold you back from striving for your highest. To face death head-on is to come to know the meaning of what is put forth in the Bible: "O Death, where is thy sting? O Grave, where is thy victory?" Through this process of looking death straight in the eye, you will come to conquer life's last great obstacle.

LIFE IS ABOUT FULFILLING
YOUR FANTASIES

As you are in fear of not surviving, you work hard trying to live a disciplined life of self-imposed deprivation. You do your duty, work at achieving success, attempt to bring glory to yourself, your family, your nation—even to your ancestors. In fact, deprivation derived from the instinct of survival is no virtue. Life never means to deprive you. Living well means living a life of fulfilling your righteous fantasies.

Marie is a fifty-three year old professional woman who immigrated from France to the United States thirty years ago. Recently, she was offered a rent-free house in France for two months if she could afford the time away from her work. Although she had visited the country from time to time for business conferences, she longed to have the opportunity to repatriate for a while to the land of her youth and childhood. However, the high cost of hotel rooms had always prohibited her staying longer than a week for each of her past visits.

Now, facing an opportunity to fulfill her greatest fantasy, she hesitated. She thought about her already overstretched workload and the projects she was supposed to have initiated over the past year that she had been putting off because of lack of time. There was no way she could spare two months for leisure. In her mind, there was a tug-of-war pulling between her reality and her fantasy, survival and living.

"If I go to France," she thought, "I can fulfill my fantasy. If I stay home, I can progress in my work."

Marie imagined the fun she could have in France—the food, the wine, the music, the smell of the air, and the joy of speaking French every day. The conflict in her heart was that she had always placed her career before everything else. Now she desperately tried to find a 'legitimate' reason to go.

She thought of the possibility of visiting some potential business partners, but she could not justify to herself that she needed two months for that. Finally, she decided to erase from her mind the idea of going to France—she could not afford two months of her time just to fulfill fantasies.

When she shared her decision with a friend, the friend gave this advice: "You weren't born to work yourself to death. You were born to fulfill your desire for experiences. To live well, which includes fulfilling your righteous fantasies, leads you to complete your desire to experience life. To your soul, the fulfilling of fantasies is as important as accomplishing your career goals. It is wrong to die without satisfying those fantasies." The light clicked on for Marie. She packed her bags and went.

I met Marie recently in France. She told me that miraculously during her stay in France she ran into her old high school lover whose wife had just passed away. Now they are married and her job was moved to France permanently by her American company. This story proves what Voltaire said, "All good things happen to those of cheerful disposition." Life was meant to be easy and fun.

CONCLUSION

When you are willing to not survive, the static of uneasiness flees while harmony and calmness set in. Without mastering this, your emotions are an eternal yo-yo flying between the fear of failure and the desire for victory.

The Rainmaker has to *not* care about whether he is able to bring rain or not. Nor can the Rainmaker care about his professional reputation. Thoughts such as whether he will have to give the money back, or if his wife will leave him, can never enter his mind. The Rainmaker knows the secret of life and death. Life has ways of always taking care of itself, including the fact of whether the village will ever see rain again. He focuses on bringing harmony into himself and lets God bring the rain. He is at peace within himself and the world. By trying to make rain, he has to be willing to not make rain.

For the Rainmaker, unless he is detached from life itself, he cannot have the full power of freedom to do his job, creating rain. As long as his survival is bound up in his need to produce the 'proper' result, he is unable to bring harmony to the village. When he is attached to making rain—the idea of a job well done—he is on the treadmill of fear. He is out of harmony with universe. The ultimate detachment is rooted in not fearing death. When you are willing to not survive, you will thrive.

SUMMARY

- Life is pointless unless, through living a life of devotion to duty, we drop a little piece of mortality in exchange for divinity.

- Life is full of contradiction. In order to live well, one must conquer the fear of death.

- If we knew we were going to die soon, we would not be so concerned about making mistakes. Even if we made mistakes, the consequences would not be so awful, because death would come to our rescue.

- Life is about fulfilling your fantasies.

- Consider the benefits when one spends time contemplating the state of death.

  1. It keeps us focused on what is truly important in our daily lives.

  2. It puts problems in their proper perspective so they seem less troublesome.

  3. It decreases our stress level.

  4. It focuses the heart on love. We come to know that the purpose of living is to know love.

  5. It helps us to calm our minds.

  6. It intensifies our connectedness with our Creator.

7. It focuses us to act with more discrimination when the temptations of greed and questionable opportunities present themselves.

8. It cultivates the profound state of detachment from loss and gain. It gives us equal vision about temporary success and failure.

9. It fortifies within us the freedom and courage to do what we are supposed to do—not what is expedient and comfortable.

10. It crystallizes within us the conviction that the purpose of life is to prepare us for the moment of death; that we are accountable and everything we do matters.

11. It gives us fearlessness, for the source of all fear is rooted in the fear of death.

12. Most of all, it will break our survival mode so that we can enjoy and thrive in our life and career.

- In order to make rain, our Rainmaker must be willing to not make rain.

- In order to create a harmonious inner environment, you need to be willing to not survive. When you are willing to not survive, you will thrive.

Secret 1.3:
Surrender reveals your destiny

We and God have business with each other;
and in opening ourselves to His influence
our deepest destiny is fulfilled.

The universe, at those parts of it
which our personal being constitutes,
takes a turn genuinely for the better
or for the worse in proportion as
each one of us fulfills or evades God's demands.

— William James

Confucius said: "When you are fifty years old, you should know your destiny." Fifty years old is figurative; you can be five, thirty, or sixty years old. Or you can be eighty years old and clueless about your destiny. Confucius is really communicating the concept that, if you have lived long enough, you should have made enough mistakes and accumulated enough sense to surrender to the will of Heaven. Only then, will you be able to see your destiny as Heaven intends it.

Our Rainmaker, before he found his God-ordained occupation, he too made numerous wrong turns in his effort towards pursuing his righteous destiny—but exactly how can you know your destiny—you cannot just eat rice or pasta for fifty years and earn the merit of knowing your destiny.

THE CLASHING OF THE AGENDAS

There are two agendas prevalent in this world: God's and yours. Often these two will clash with each other. When what we want our life to be is different than that of our intended destiny, the universal will creates road blocks. Although we may fight with all of our might in an attempt to turn the outcome to our desires, the universal will prevails. Out of desperation, we surrender.

GIVING UP AND GIVING IN

Giving in to the will of Heaven does not mean doing nothing and just accepting life as you find it. It means using your God-given ability, talent, and strength to do all you can to bring about a better life for yourself and others. You accept divine guidance instead of insisting on your preset notions about how things ought to be. You accept with wisdom the validity of the way things are.

Giving in by surrendering to the guidance of the divine intelligence is quite different from giving up into defeat.

Surrendering to divine guidance requires strength, possibility thinking, discrimination, and wisdom. Conversely, surrendering to defeat requires nothing more than despair, hopelessness, devastation, becoming overwhelmed by life, and finally, tossing in the towel.

True surrender comes by knowing God's grand design beyond the superficial, mundane level, and thus opening up to and accepting divine guidance, allowing it to affect your life in an astoundingly positive way.

KICKING AND SCREAMING ALL THE WAY

Surrendering to the Divine Will is not an easy task. Most of us go through life furiously fighting for what we think is best for us. Yet, through kindness, our Maker drags us along despite our objections. Adults see a child's idea of the 'good life' as pure foolishness—a life with no school, no homework, and plenty of pizzas, hamburgers, candy bars, and cookies while watching television and listening to rock-and-roll all day.

Yet, we adults are no different in the eyes of the Divine. Each of us also has a definite idea of what the 'good life' means. When things do not turn out to fit our mental pictures, we are devastated by our disappointment.

CELEBRATING A BROKEN HEART

Humans will do anything to avoid having our hearts broken. Yet, only when the heart is broken and the resistive ego cracked can we let in the light of wisdom. For those extraordinary people whom God has intended to exalt to the highest splendor, God Himself will raise the hammer, crack their hearts, and take residence within.

THERE IS NO FAILURE, ONLY DIVINE REDIRECTION

At times, we are out of tune with the grand blueprint for our intended destiny, and sometimes we desire to go into places where we don't belong. The universal force then repeatedly pushes us back to the centre of the road so that we may start over again in the proper direction to fulfill better our personal destiny. Each time we have a reversal and start again, the ignorant of this world label our actions a failure.

In 1970, one year after I immigrated to the United States, I needed a job because I hadn't married a rich Chinese. As I took inventory of myself, I realized two of my assets were that I could speak a little English and a lot of Chinese. At the time, the job of airline stewardess was considered very glamorous. That I could fly between the United States and Asia and live both as a Chinese as well as an American appealed to me. This was the most perfect job I could dream of. Then, Northwest Airlines was the only U.S. airline flying to Asia. I telephoned and requested an application. Until now, I still haven't heard from them.

The experience of rejection was devastating. I was so naive that, to maximize my competitive edge, I enrolled in a mail-order stewardess school which put me in debt for two years. After failing to become a stewardess, I took a job at the local drugstore as a minimum wage cashier. As I look back, I thank God that Northwest Airlines didn't respond, otherwise you might have met me on a flight serving you tea.

In 1983, I was at a crossroads in my career again. I applied for a sales position with IBM. After an one-hour interview, they decided not to hire me. Ten years later, in 1993, I delivered a keynote address, speaking to one thousand of IBM's top sales associates at their annual acknowledgment conference in Bali.

In fact, life is a circle within a circle in which there exists these relative incidents along the way that are erroneously identified as failure and success. Each failure is a progression forward within the grand framework of our inevitable, complete success. Every disappointment, every failure is God's way of guiding you in silence to your intended destiny. "Child, you are going the wrong way. This is not the path to your destiny" or "You should do it differently; your execution does not fit your talent. Polish your skills." God says, "In spite of your objections, I shall direct you to your destiny." There are no failures, only Divine redirection.

DESTINY REVEALS ITSELF IN THREE PHASES

Since human beings are resistant creatures, we do not give up our agenda until we engage God in an arm-wrestling match. When we surrender to God's arm, we win. On the other hand, when we win the arm-wrestling, we lose. For those who have put up a gallant fight and won their battle with God, they forever remain in darkness about their destiny. These people generally work hard and earn their money, but without satisfaction. For most people, destiny reveals itself through the following three phases:

The first phase: you are hungry

It all starts when you feel dissatisfied with life. Without a sufficiently large appetite for life, there is no motivation toward action. If you do not act, nothing happens—you vegetate and die. Even the simple act of eating requires the will to action.

In the initial phase of your pursuit of personal success, you will find that you are enthusiastically motivated. Your actions are driven by a self-centred desire, and they vibrate with a single voice of "I want, I want, I want." This phase is like crude oil fueling a diesel engine: it's loud, it's powerful, but it's not refined.

By being hungry, you will obtain certain objects of your desires. The power of hunger will motivate you to exercise your will. Like an enthusiastic bull charging forward, you will be off to a good start. At this stage, you are winning the wrestling match. Your score is one; God, zero.

However, when you have lived long enough and enjoyed a certain amount of success in fulfilling your desires, you often discover that you are not totally happy at this phase. In fact, you may find that you are more confused and miserable now than you ever have been. This all happens to you because God is good and kind, and you have been extremely lucky. It is a sign that the Universe is taking a personal interest in you and readjusting your course so that you may achieve way beyond your present meagre successes.

The second phase: the turning point

Phase two is often caused by some kind of dramatic turning point in one's life, such as a personal tragedy, the loss of a loved one, professional setbacks, or financial failure. As a matter of fact, whatever hurts you the most will happen. Motivated by your experience of pain, you begin your inner quest.

All of those pleasures that you thought were so much fun and that you pursued with such great zest and zeal suddenly become tasteless and dull. Your attention shifts from the blind pursuit of glory and vanity to the sincere attempt to enter into the hidden inner kingdom that you have heard of through the writings of the great ones and that are alluded to in the songs of poets.

When you begin this inner search, you often discover that your way is blocked. Upon finding that your chief impediment is you, you become overwhelmed by your own character defects and pettiness. It is like being in a room where there is no sunlight and therefore you see no dirt. When the drapes are pulled back a little, the sunlight pours in and suddenly you discover that everything in the room is covered with dust and the air is filled with dust particles. What is staring back at you is your own inadequacy and self-doubt. This is the phase that ignites the rocket of transformation. However, this is also the most dangerous and threatening phase.

Movement from phase one to phase two happens because of God's grace. It does not require your intervention. God shoves your face into your own dirt. At this point, the score of the game is God, one; you, one. Now it is up to you to pull yourself up from phase two into three. So many people get stuck at phase two, defeated by it, and end up as the proverbial successful failures.

Phase two is not sent to defeat you. Rather, it is the cleansing process you must pass through so that you can proceed on to phase three and experience a much higher, refined degree of success. There are success stories that we encounter every day that can be ascribed to temporary good luck. However, no person who has enjoyed true and lasting success, who has left a legacy of progress and goodness for the world, has ever been spared from walking through the dark tunnel of phase two; God wins, you lose. Now you are on your way to fulfilling your destiny.

The third phase: becoming clear about your destiny

What is supposed to be yours, no one can take away, delay, or stop from coming to you. You know that your success does not depend on certain individuals or circumstances, but on the ever-generous pouring forth from the cornucopia of God's desire for your happiness as you remain attuned to Him. You know that destiny is your master as well as your servant.

You perform your duty in harmony with the Divine will, and therefore you can disregard the state of the moment-to-moment results. You know that everything you have done will eventually and inevitably lead toward the ultimate completeness of your material and spiritual rewards. At this point, your score total is one; God, two. You lose, therefore, you win.

This is a highly evolved state that may seem unusual or impossible when one is stuck in a prior phase. Be assured, however, that this is the state of mind that the women and men of destiny share and the state that lies dormant in each human soul, waiting to be activated.

GEORGE WASHINGTON'S JOURNEY

George Washington's life followed exactly the three phases described above. In the lives of most people, the three phases are not so well defined and clearly distinguishable; there are inevitable overlaps. In Washington's life, these phases happened in a clear-cut, precise order.

Whether you attended grade school in the United States or elsewhere, the story of young George Washington chopping down the cherry tree is ubiquitous. This story gave Washington such an aura of holiness that we mere mortals felt inadequate when our virtues did not compare to the pure seed of greatness that had been planted in the breast of this extraordinary child. In fact, according to historians, this story is a fiction manufactured by a clergyman to inspire the children who attended his Sunday School classes to follow the path of honesty. The real story of the real man named George Washington is a tale of quite a different type.

The life story of George Washington reveals a man who evolved from a swindler to an icon who finally embodied true, altruistic greatness. As we get in touch with the human side of Washington's life story, our admiration is not tarnished. Instead, it expands into the realization of how truly great was the stature of this Father of America. As Abraham Lincoln said of Washington, "To add brightness to the sun or glory to the name of Washington is impossible."

Phase One: George was hungry

Destiny's setbacks

When Washington was eleven, his father died. His two elder half-brothers, Lawrence and Augustine, received most of their father's estate. Also, they were both sent to England for the best of educations. The teenager, George, without the edge of wealth and a proper formal education, set out to make his mark on the world stage.

When George was sixteen, Lawrence invited him to live at Mount Vernon. Lawrence, then thirty, was a Major in the Virginia militia and served as a member of the House of Burgesses, the governing body of that colony. He had married into one of the wealthiest families in the territory. Young George found the lavish lifestyle of his brother Lawrence, much to his liking. Washington was proud of his brother and felt that he, too, deserved everything that his brother had— the status of gentleman, copious wealth, and a well-landed estate. Nothing was more valued than the attainment of this coveted status, in the life of an eighteenth-century Virginian.

Young George conducted himself with great maturity. While he lived at Mount Vernon and enjoyed the life of a Virginian squire, his young mind was busy mapping his path to wealth and designing his future so that he could continue living in the manner to which he was fast becoming accustomed.

Collecting the symbols of success

George was obsessed in these younger years with the idea of being a proper 'gentleman.' Even in his early years, he had started to collect the 'symbols' of the gentleman.

To be a gentleman, one must have a gentlemanly occupation: In Washington's time, being a land surveyor was an important and prestigious position, equal in stature to that of physician or clergyman. In 1749, at the age of seventeen, George passed his examination and officially filed his commission as a land surveyor.

A gentleman must have land—the more, the better: Working as a surveyor, George was well paid. By the time he was twenty, he owned 2,008 acres of the most fertile land in the area. Being a surveyor, he was naturally able to pick for himself the best parcels of land.

Washington's acreage was not all obtained through honest work. At the beginning of the French and Indian War, the governor of Virginia, in order to entice the colonists to fight, promised land to all of the enlisted men. The offer did not include the officers, on whom, as gentlemen, the governor was counting to serve, out of their sense of aristocratic honour.

By the end of the eight-year French and Indian War, a new governor had arrived who was not familiar with the details of the previous governor's promise. George and his fellow officers conspired together and were able to change the old proclamation that had granted the land to the enlisted men into granting it to the officers.

Through this cheap swindle, at a great cost to those men whom he had commanded, Washington obtained an additional 20,000 acres of prime fertile land.

A gentleman must have a gentleman's wife: At the age of twenty-seven, George married a woman truly worthy of being a gentleman's wife: Martha Curtis, a twenty-eight year old lady who happened to be the wealthiest widow in Virginia. Possessing money and position, she had all the apparatuses of prestige that George had always chased. Through this marriage, George gained the status of a true gentleman.

A gentleman must have gentlemanly company: Armed with a gentleman's wife, Washington began entertaining his neighbours at Mount Vernon. He gave lavish parties, inviting those who could help him promote himself and expedite his ambitions. He was constantly pursuing the opportunity to rub elbows with the rich, the famous, and the powerful.

A gentleman must have political and social position: Following in the footsteps of his brother, Lawrence, George ran for the House of Burgesses. He lost the first time because, on the day of the election, he did not serve liquor to the voters, as was custom. The second time he ran, he made sure that the bar was generously stocked and open to all voters. It worked liked a charm; he was elected to the governing body of the colony of Virginia.

A gentleman must wear the red coat: Washington served in the Virginia militia at the rank of Major and was eventually promoted to Commander. However, the rank of Commander in the Virginia militia was nothing compared to becoming a British officer—the true mark of a gentleman. Throughout his life, George had craved a position in the British army.

Washington's only military education had consisted of reading two art-of-war books and, in his spare time, taking fencing lessons. However, this lack of formal military training never stopped him from desiring to wear the distinguished red coat of the British officer.

After repeated requests, and subsequent rejections, Washington gave up the idea of becoming a British officer, convinced that he was being discriminated against because he was a colonist. This obsessive desire to be a British officer played a major role in the shaping of his destiny.

Washington's character defects

In the first phase his of life, Washington was totally ignorant of his numerous personality defects.

His vanity: When Washington received his first military assignment in 1754 during the French and Indian War, he thought this was his big chance to be recognized by the 'powers that be.' Washington established Fort Necessity in the Great Meadows at the Forks of Ohio. At the first rainstorms, flooding had George and his men up to their knees in mud and water, which compelled them to give up the fort and surrender to the French.

Washington signed the surrender document which was written in French. Not being conversant in that language, he did not realize that he had signed an admission of guilt that, in a previous battle, he had assassinated a French diplomat after that gentleman had surrendered to him and was being held as his prisoner.

The document referred to an incident precipitated by an Indian chief who, while fighting on the side of the English and assisting Washington, charged without warning into the circle of French prisoners and bashed in the head of the diplomat with his tomahawk.

In order to reply to the charges and offer the correct explanation, Washington would have had to admit that he was not knowledgeable in French. Since it was the mark of a true English gentleman, in those days, to be able to speak and write French fluently, he would not admit that.

His habit of blaming others: Clearly, Washington's first chance to be recognized as a great commander had turned out badly. In his defence, he promptly blamed the officer whom he had picked to be his translator for his poor translation job. Of course, since Washington could not read French, he had no business picking a French translator. He then blamed his superior who had sent him to do battle at the Forks.

Throughout his life, when circumstances did not transpire according to his vision, Washington would find others to blame. When he met with failure and difficulties, he would always feel victimized and double-crossed.

His craving for recognition: At the age of twenty, Washington rode to Williamsburg for an audience with Governor Dinwiddie. There, he requested that he be appointed to the Virginia militia at the rank of major. For a man with no military training, what he was asking was a tall order, and his request was turned down. Eventually, the rank of major was granted to George when he was given the peaceful and least strategic portion of southern Virginia to defend.

Even then, his title was not given based upon his merit. It came about because of his relationship with the notable Lord Thomas Fairfax, a distant relative by marriage. Furthermore, Governor Dinwiddie was a business partner with George's brother, Lawrence. Due to this, no one took Washington seriously at the regiment. Even the junior officers did not want to obey him.

Phase Two: Despair

In 1775, Washington represented Virginia at the Continental Congress in Philadelphia. The focus of the discussion was taxation without representation and the British occupation.

Washington did not come to the meeting without his own agenda. He was the only delegate in the hall who dressed in the heroic military uniform of a general—one that he designed and had tailored for himself, distinguished epaulettes and all.

It is said that before others can perceive you as fit for the role in life you wish to play, you must first dress the part, act the part, and become the part. Now Washington saw the opportunity to fulfill his deepest desire. He thought that if the members of the Congress saw him in this uniform, they would see him as the man best qualified to be the Commander of the Army of the Continental Congress.

Just as Washington had anticipated, the delegates realized he was exactly what they needed. He was young enough (forty-three); he was experienced in battle (mostly in defeat); he was on the right side of political compromise—a soldier from Virginia at a time when the Congress needed to persuade the Southern colonies to join in this freedom fight; and he had his own uniform.

Historians call Washington a great actor. I call him an exceptional salesman. He sold believability and vision. After all, great salesmen are always excellent actors.

A time for fear

George was soon on the road to Boston, carrying the commission papers that gave him command over the hastily forming Continental Army. All of his life, Washington had craved the recognition bestowed upon him by the Congress. Now the reality hit home. As he looked at himself in brutal honesty, he saw only a tobacco farmer; who knew how to grow quality tobacco. However, to face well-trained, professional fighting men, he had to admit to himself that he knew little of the art of war.

Arriving in Boston, his worst fears took flesh. Where he had hoped to find the great soldiers of a revolution ready to liberate America, he found only an unkempt, ragtag bunch of greenhorn farmers, trained to raise crops and cattle, not to kill men on the battlefield. He greatly despaired. How could he lead this herd of sheep to be slaughtered by the trained, professional soldiers of Britain, the greatest conquering army in the world?

Mirror of his inadequacy

The British sailed to New York to engage Washington's army. The battles fought in New York showed Washington that his fears were well justified. His military training (from the two books he had read) proved quite inadequate. His poorly trained army was easy pickings for the crack British troops. Receiving their first taste of real battle—the blood, the gore, the screams of the dying—many of his soldiers deserted.

Washington entered a state of depression. He saw himself not as a great general but as a fake. This defeat on the battle-field was a reflection of the defeat he felt within himself at his attempt to become someone of great importance. Now there were no likely suspects available for him to blame. Previously, he had always found a convenient scapegoat; here, in his greatest defeat, he stood utterly alone.

Battling with the generals

To add to his myriad problems, he was forced to fight battles on two fronts: one against the British and the other against his own generals. Since most of his generals had been trained and had served tours of duty in the British army, they thought this bucolic upstart an interloper and a fool—inadequate to com-mand a herd of cows, much less a distinguished group of military tacticians such as themselves. They conspired to remove him by surreptitiously sending Congress venomous reports requesting that he be replaced, while at the same time they openly defied his orders and fought him at every turn.

Despair

By the end of 1776, the situation had become so hopeless and desperate that Washington had to consider the possibility of running out west to hide. In a letter to his cousin, he wrote, "I see the impossibility of serving with reputation. I was never in such unhappiness since I was born." In a letter to his younger brother, Jack, he was even more honest and frank, "I think the game is pretty near over."

Phase Three:
Becoming clear about his destiny

Defeating the demons within

More horrible to Washington than defeat or death was the thought that he would have to accept the reality of being a nobody, a nothing, a fake. He had struggled all of his life trying to prove to himself and others that he was a man of importance and worthy of respect. Now the mirror of self-reflection was facing him; the pain of defeat was forcing him to take a long, hard look at himself.

He realized that if one expects to be respected, one must respect himself first. He must be a man of true substance— something more than the stuff and symbols he had gathered around himself for the purpose of being respectable. Before Washington could defeat the British, he had to defeat the demons of his own mind. Before he could achieve victory over the world, he had to triumph over himself.

Turning inward

In December 1776, Washington was in serious trouble. The enlistment time of his soldiers was up, and they were about to go home. So far, he had seen nothing but defeat. In desper-ation, George Washington, the man, turned inward to consult with George Washington, the spirit.

Dreading the loss of a reputation that had taken him a lifetime to build, Washington sank into the agony in the pit of his soul. In this condition of resignation, his mind stopped racing and became still. He became detached and, in this state, discerned the true meaning of honour and recognition.

They had nothing to do with all the symbols he had collected, such as the large house, land, and social and political status. They had only to do with whether a man is willing to do God's bidding—to fulfill the duty and role his Maker has assigned to him in this life.

George discovers the axiom of inner completeness

By being in touch with his own spirit, Washington was, in turn, touched by God. He saw that his blind, vigorous pursuit of becoming a respectable gentleman was rooted in his lack of the sense of completeness within himself.

George knew he could not win the war by fighting for all the wrong reasons. The things that had been so important— reputation, status, a royal commission—were as insignificant as not being able to read French. From here, he could see unto the far horizon of the future, and he saw that the role that had been entrusted to him was so grand, even death would be a meagre price to pay.

Once he had given up the burden of vanity, his mind was sharply focused. Every cell of his body and brain were aligned with his soul's cry of victory for this most noble of causes. Now he would fight effectively because it was his God-assigned duty to fight. It was his destiny to win this war for the noble, fledgling republic struggling to be born on the shores of the continent called America.

With the turning around of Washington's inner state, so too turned the fate of the American Revolution. On that freezing Christmas Eve in 1776, Washington single-handedly altered the course of American history.

The turning point

With twenty-four hundred men, he crossed the Delaware River
in the midst of a snowstorm to mount a sneak attack. His battle
cry was, "Death or Victory." He and his men were grimly determined to turn the war around or die in the attempt.

That Christmas eve was the beginning of the transmuting
of defeat into victory. Turning from the rules of traditional
warfare to the use of deceptive tactics, Washington arrived
with his men at the enemy camp at 3:00 in the morning. The
enemy, Hessian mercenaries sleeping off a night of unbridled
drunken revelry, were unprepared. It was a complete rout.

The birth of a true leader

In April 1781, the British were attacking in Virginia and had
their cannons trained on Washington's estate at Mount
Vernon. Thomas Jefferson, then the governor of Virginia, told
Washington to come home and mount a defence for his home
and state. Sitting at his camp on the Hudson River, Washington declined. He had grown dispassionate about small vic-
tories. He knew that the pivotal point of his military operation
was where he was, up north. His intention was to win the
war, not the battle.

Washington had become totally unconcerned about his
possessions at Mount Vernon. He removed his identification
from his beloved estate in Virginia; he was no longer a Virginian. Washington was now a man of destiny, a citizen of the
American republic, the future country for whose birth he was
selflessly fighting.

The fight between Washington's revolutionary army and
the British Empire was a war that tested the endurance of
both participants' to the limits. To win, Washington knew that

63

he had to outlast England's appetite for war. Washington was aware that he could not really defeat this superior enemy in the battlefield; he knew that he must outlast them by enduring longer and greater hardships than they were willing to.

Washington and his American revolutionary army sustained their spirit through to the last significant battle of the American Revolution—the three-week siege of Yorktown—and there, bowing to the superior desire, will, and purpose of the colonists, the British army surrendered.

Embracing destiny

On 15 March, 1783, he was in his quarters, furiously preparing a speech powerful enough to stop a civil war. His generals were not willing to hand over the victory and power to a Continental Congress that had done nothing but lie to them throughout the course of the war.

Now the generals wanted to storm Congress, guns loaded, to demand their back pay. They intended to create a form of dictatorial government and declare Washington the king. George Washington, the man who had been driven totally by his search for the status of gentleman and the commission of an English officer, now had the opportunity to be king, an equal to George the Third. But the Washington of yesterday was no longer alive in this new Washington.

Standing before his men, Washington read his carefully prepared speech and the letter he had just received from the Congress, which promised once again to pay their back wages. As he concluded, he looked into their eyes and saw that they had not been convinced. The powers of persuasion, spirit, and eloquence that had induced his men to follow him through freezing winters, starvation, and bloody battles failed him in the glow of victory.

The air was heavy and suffocating. The crowd of soldiers pressed closer, all eyes upon him. Washington stopped. He then did an extraordinary thing. Slowly, he removed a pair of glasses from his coat pocket. His men had never seen him wearing glasses; they were shocked at this sign of frailty in their invincible leader.

Washington looked up and said, "Gentlemen, you will forgive the spectacles. Not only have I grown grey in your service; now I find myself going blind." With these few words, he touched their hearts and brought tears to the eyes of these rock-hard, seasoned fighting men. The glasses symbolized how he had given up everything—his youth, his life, his fortune— for the cause of victory, that by betraying their noble cause through rash action, they would also betray him who had given all he had.

At this moment, as he referred to his eyesight and his personal sacrifice for the revolution, he was reminding his men of the price they had already paid for the ideal of the Republic. The Republic was greater than the Congress that hadn't paid them. His gesture also reminded his men how together they had contributed to the founding of their new nation and that it wasn't the time to forsake their destiny. By abandoning the kingship, he embraced his divine destiny in history.

Historians regard this scene as an extraordinary political performance. I see it as beyond performance. This was the moment that George Washington, the man, merged with his destiny to become the Father of the Nation. Most people thought that Washington had a flawless character. As we have seen, he had just as many human flaws and carried as much emotional baggage as anyone else. Yet, in spite of himself, his character defects, by learning from life's trials and tribu- lations, he ultimately evolved into a heroic man of destiny.

THE BEGINNING OF SURRENDER

Dawn plays her lute before the gate of darkness,
and is content to vanish when the sun comes out.

— Rabindranath Tagore

Surrender is the essential element necessary for moving from
the second phase, the *turning point*, to the third phase, *becoming clear about your destiny*. The caveat is, true surrender
always comes with a big price tag. God never means to hurt
you, but when God puts out His hand to redirect you to the
high road, you often feel the sting of His touch. In the Hindu
scriptures, the story is told of Lord Shiva stirring up the
ocean of human consciousness. When the poison sediment of
evil tendencies, that had been accumulating over the years at
the bottom of that mental sea, surfaced, the previously crystal-
clear water became deeply clouded. In a move to save humankind from folly, Lord Shiva drank the murky, lethal, deposit-
filled liquid, and His throat turned blue when the poison
lodged there.

In this story Shiva represents our human spirit stirring
up the submerged dirt in our mental sea. If we do not deal
with our subconscious shortcomings, we end up living in an
ignorantly blissful state. All we see within ourselves is goodness. In this state of personal self-righteousness, we, and those
who agree with us and believe like us, are 'right,' and the rest
of the world is 'wrong.'

When phase two, the turning point, comes, we are forced
to look at ourselves with an objective, critical eye and see
what is really there. We then disturb the quicksand sediments
of our mind and, as happened when Lord Shiva stirred the
ocean of human consciousness, our dirt begins to surface. This
is the beginning of the inner transformation, the beginning of
the battle for surrender.

FOUR STEPS TO SURRENDER

To say it briefly and clearly,
so that there may be no doubt:
God in His faithfulness
gives each man what is best for him.

— Meister Eckhart

Everyone's life contains a certain amount of unexpected tragedy, and we find that when one surrenders to Heaven's will, magically, all turns out for the best. Even death and financial disaster can bring triumph and success. The intensity of life's dramas may vary, but the steps that lead to attaining this noble state of divine surrender are the same.

1. Desperation: everything seems out of control. Nothing goes the way it is 'supposed' to. You are doing everything you can, trying to control and fix it. Even with all of your intelligence, determination and strength, you cannot reverse the set course.

2. Detachment versus giving up: out of desperation you want to give up. At this stage some simply quit and cave in, never to move out of the state of defeat. They are stuck there unto the grave, while others gain the wisdom of detachment. The difference between the state of detachment and the act of giving up is that people who are detached are not crushed by life's setbacks: they don't give up. They discover the hidden treasure in the hopeless situation and then redirect their energies to follow the current, swimming with the force of the waves. For those who give up out of hopelessness, they stop struggling and, yet, still hold on to their old picture of how life ought to be and continue moaning about why it is not.

3. Witness: when you are detached, you enter into the state of witness. While you are adjusting your course, forsaking your old ways, relearning the rhythm of the forces occurring around you and engaging in positive actions, another part of you is witnessing the rise and fall of the human drama without enmity or affection.

When I first experienced this state of 'don't care so much,' I was quite alarmed. I asked, "How can I get ahead if part of me seems to not really care? If I really don't care that much about gain and loss, how can I motivate myself to work with enthusiasm?" Then I noticed that when I 'don't care' a great deal about the outcome or the process, my performance is raised to a new level of excellence with clarity and ease. True excellence is not born out of struggle and desperation, rather it comes from the place of calm that is born out of surrender.

4. Surrender: when you surrender unto the power of the Almighty and embrace the true essence of 'Let Thy Will be Done,' you perform your duty without agitation and desire, yet, your actions will benefit yourself and millions of others. You will become the earthly vehicle for that heavenly will.

THE PATH TO OVERCOMING EMOTIONAL TURBULENCE

While you are battling for surrender, the following points can help to alleviate the pain of riding your emotional roller coaster:

1. Avoid suppression

Drop the twin burdens of failure and success. This does not mean that you are not to experience your emotions of joy upon achieving, or of agony upon defeat.

A friend of mine recently brought up the question about how the Japanese tend to suppress their emotions. The root of this behaviour is to be found within the Buddhist tradition. In spiritual pursuits, the seeker should be able to totally detach his emotion from the joy of gain and the agony of loss. To the samurai warrior, the highest ancient social class and the role model for Japan's present-day populace, expressing the emotions of joy or sadness was considered inferior. A samurai was expected to view joy and sadness as equal and remain aloof from both.

However, as many noble ideas suffer upon contact with the human mind, misconceptions have occurred, and well-intentioned traditions have been distorted. Instead of striving to achieve an inner detachment from their emotions, many Japanese practice an outer suppression of their emotions, to the detriment of their health.

2. Walk through the dark valley

The sublime indifference to one's high and low emotions is often reached by a willingness to walk through the dark valley of the broken heart, to examine unabashed the core of our pain and agony. While we are acting out our agonies and ecstasies, part of us is just watching the show. We are the audience as well as the actor. With practice, playing the two roles simultaneously will come naturally.

By watching and witnessing our reactions to events, we gain an understanding of ourselves. In time, we place less and less importance on our highs and lows, joys and sorrows, gains and losses.

3. Let your fingers do the walking

Try writing down how you feel. If you have had the experience of writing down your emotions, you know that often what you intend to write may be very different from what you actually end up writing. You will discover that your fingers have a mind of their own. You might think you know how you feel until you see your mind directing your fingers to write things that you never thought were in your head.

4. Nothing in this world happens by accident

One thing is certain: life is ever-changing. Through change, nature evolves and human wisdom progresses. Nothing in this world is an accident. Every seemingly insignificant event hides a profound mystery that is waiting to be discovered. Not a single leaf dares fall without God's permission. Through unexpected incidents, the universe tries to teach you something. Learn the lessons.

5. Celebrate a broken heart

Rejoice and celebrate each time your heart is broken. Only when your heart is broken can the light enter. Not until you have felt the pain of suffering can you know how others suffer. This is where you learn empathy. This is when others can look into your eyes, the windows of the soul, and see texture, wisdom, compassion and refinement. After the experience of a broken heart you became more beautiful and more attractive to the world.

CONCLUSION

The glory that is yours cannot be locked away from you; defeat can only come from leaving the track before the race has been won. When you realize that, wherever you are, you are in the right place.

Do not envy others who have achieved Phase One success at a very young age. What goes up must come down, and what is down will come up. This is the law of karma. Play the cards that the Great Gambler has dealt you. Life is a school. Unless you complete your lessons at each phase, you are not able to move forward. One's life becomes repetitive by dealing with the same old tired lessons. Some will never arrive at the third phase during this lifetime; they will only toy around between the first and second phases.

However, for those who are willing to grow, the Divine hands are willing and eager to interfere and throw you forward, in spite of yourself. Attack the circumstances in which God has placed you with diligence and courage. Life is designed for you to win, even though the odds against you seem insurmountable. Like Washington, our meagre desires can also ignite explosive transformations into the highest of ideals and destinies.

Life is designed for you to win in spite of yourself. Life unfolds like a fine wine. If you begin with good grapes, cultivate them with great care, agitate the grapes, and store their juice in good oak barrels, you will harvest a superb wine. Every step along the way is important. Nothing is lost. Every apparent dead-end and misstep will ultimately turn out to have been necessary.

When questioned, "How did you discover your destiny?", the Rainmaker replied that he had simply asked the universal Being to make clear his way. He affirmed, "I will will, I will reason, I will act. Guide Thou my reason, will, and activities in the right direction that what I shall do is in accordance with the way of health, wealth and happiness. Such is the way to my destiny."

SUMMARY

- In order to know how to relax into success, you must learn how to relax into great disappointments and pain. Until you can understand the essence of surrender, you will never feel at ease with life's ups and downs.

- There are two agendas in this world: God's and yours. Often these two will clash with each other.

- Surrender occurs when you find your personal agenda clashing with God's, and you accept divine guidance instead of insisting on your preset notions about how things ought to be. You accept with wisdom the validity of the way things are.

- Surrender does not mean doing nothing and just accepting life as you find it. It means using your God-given ability, talent, and strength to do all you can to bring about a better life for yourself and others.

- True surrender comes by knowing God's grand design beyond the superficial, mundane level, and thus opening up to and accepting divine guidance, allowing it to affect your life in an astoundingly positive way.

- Surrendering to the guidance of the divine intelligence is quite different from giving up or giving in to defeat.

- Surrendering to divine guidance requires strength, possibility thinking, discrimination, and wisdom.

- Harvesting through surrender is finding joy in the process of living.

- Through surrender, the fruit of self-enrichment and personal growth allows your highest good to unfold naturally. Thereby, one is led to a fuller satisfaction in all pursuits.

- Surrendering to the divine will is not an easy task. Most of us go through the experience fighting what is often best for us. Yet, through kindness, our Maker drags us along despite our objections.

- The path to overcoming emotional turbulence:

    1. Avoid suppression: Drop the twin burdens of failure and success. Strive to achieve an inner detachment from your emotions.

    2. Walk through the dark valley: The path to arriving at a sublime indifference about one's high and low emotions is often reached by a willingness to walk through the dark valley of the broken heart.

    3. Let your fingers do the walking: If you have had the experience of writing down your emotions, you know that often what you intend to write may be very different from what you actually end up writing.

    4. Nothing in this world happens by accident: Every seemingly insignificant event hides a profound mystery that is waiting to be discovered. Not a single leaf dares fall without God's permission. Through unexpected incidents, the universe tries to teach you something. Learn the lesson.

5. Celebrate a broken heart: Humans will do anything to avoid having their hearts broken. For those extraordinary people whom God has intended to exalt to the highest splendor, God Himself will raise the hammer, crack their hearts, and take residence within.

- There is no failure, only Divine redirection.

- Destiny reveals itself in three phases:
    1. You are hungry.
    2. The turning point.
    3. Becoming clear about your destiny.

2nd Secret:
Illuminate the mind with apropos nourishment

In our attempts to reach for the stars, we must seize the mind and demand more from it. However, if we only take from the mind without feeding it with the proper nourishment, the mind rebels by becoming desperate. The mind's food is the illuminating light of wisdom. Your mind needs to be exposed to this essential while it pursues its worldly fulfillments on your behalf. Your mind asks questions and demands answers about why life turns out the way it does; what is the meaning of life? It certainly cannot just be to make more money so we can die in a fancier casket. Furthermore, what are the strategies we can employ so we can more easily achieve out of life what we want?

The Rainmaker cannot perform his job effectively if his mind is loaded with puzzles about the meaning of life and living.

Secret 2.1:

Irritation is the beginning of a good thing

In order to achieve the state of being that the Rainmaker did, we must first truthfully acknowledge where we are. Through the promise of technology, life was supposed to become progressively easier for everyone. More leisure and higher productivity were expected, but for some mysterious reason, progress has not realized its original purpose. Instead, we are forced to accelerate our physical activity and mental throughput in order to keep up with the velocities of advancing technology —the fax machine, e-mail, the cellular phone, computers. Often the more techno-savvy we become, the more overwhelmed and irritated we become.

As the world swirls around us, we see the silent anguish of many courageous people who have put forth a monstrous amount of energy and yet reap meagre results. Even those who achieve the material prosperity that all strive for are beset by an uneasiness that mars their enjoyment of the fruits of their labour. Life could not be meant to irritate us only. Everything in life happens for a special purpose. Even the experience of irritation is part of the great game of self-improvement and inner-growth.

THE IRRITATED, STRESSED-OUT RAINMAKER

Before the Rainmaker acquired his power of making rain *effortlessly*, he too was an anxious intern. Like all mediocre rainmakers, his extraordinary effort and meagre results caused him to be an irritated and stressed-out rainmaker. Our Rainmaker, even though inept at creating rain early in his career, knew his irritation was the beginning of a good thing.

When one is suffering from irritation and a stress-filled life, there is no virtue to it unless the suffering is accompanied by wisdom. The Rainmaker needs to know how his suffering is contributing to his future ability as a superior rainmaker.

SEEING LIFE AS A CELESTIAL SPORT

In order to relax into life's challenges, you have to step back, take a look at the big picture, and ask yourself the serious question: If, as some cynics have said, life sucks and then we die, why should we even bother to live? When we have the answers to this question, we begin to take life's tests much more lightly. We may even begin to enjoy our daily struggle as a bundle of fun.

THE JOY OF COMPETITION

In the early 1900s, a peasant warlord in China was invited to visit a prestigious all-girl high school for which he was a major monetary supporter. When the warlord came to the school, he saw groups of girls fighting fiercely over a ball, running from one side of the court to the other, trying to put the ball into their respective baskets.

The warlord was furious and bellowed at the principal, "I gave you so much money to build a model school that would provide the best of everything for the students. Why don't you buy more balls so each of the girls can have one? Then they won't have to fight over just one ball!"

Why do two teams fight over a stupid ball, trying to move it into the end zone while they have their bodies bashed around and their spirits go through the greatest of punishments? Why do humans find it is so stimulating to watch their favourite teams strain to the limits of their endurance physically and mentally?

The fun of any competitive sport is derived from the struggle to overcome opposition. Those people with the physical ability or mental talent to compete, participate by playing the game; those who can't play, buy tickets so they can participate vicariously in the experience of the players' struggle.

The tougher the game, the better the game. The fiercer the competition, the more people enjoy it. The greater the challenge, the higher the excitement. When the game score is 95 to 10, the spectators and the players are both disappointed. When you are neck-to-neck and then win the game by only a few points, the game becomes very exhilarating.

The human spirit loves games of tough competition. Our life's encounters are identical to our competitions on the sports field. The only difference is that we think of sports competitions as games and consider business and life games as reality.

The rules of business, life and sports are all about overcoming strong opposition forces. The ball game becomes a metaphor for life. Problems occur when we forget that stress is an inevitable part of the human condition. Have fun while playing the game of your life.

NOT SO GREAT A LIFE

Pauline married the heir to one of the world's most powerful, solely-owned communications empires. Her family was featured on the television show *Life Styles of the Rich and Famous*. Pauline often expressed the wish that she would like to be poor and have nothing. She was often in the company of her working-class artist friends so that she could experience the 'fun' of their struggles. I could tell that she was truly envious of those who experienced the full scope of being a human being hustling to make ends meet.

One of my girlfriends is married to a rich businessman. She keeps bragging to me about how fortunate and lucky she is. Her life is so smooth, so trouble-free. Yet, when I look into her eyes, I see no light, no joy, no satisfaction and happiness.

What good is it to live life as a zombie? If her life is truly as good as she claims it to be, why must she expend so much effort to announce it? An old Chinese aphorism states, "Every family has a *sutra* (prayer) that is difficult to chant." You never have to envy other people. They all have their 'stuff,' which might prove to be even more difficult for you to handle than the troubles you have.

LIFE HAS KEPT ITS BARGAIN

Life's challenges are never meant to devastate you. In fact, the challenges are placed before you for your enjoyment and to remind you that life has kept its side of the bargain to keep the game fun and entertaining, as you have requested.

Imagine if you were misinformed about the rules of football and you thought you were supposed to walk leisurely across the field with the ball while everyone else on the opposite team were supposed to keep a respectable distance from you. Suddenly, when people came from all directions, attacking you and stealing your ball, you would be horrified and furious.

As you know the rules of football, you do not mind the attack. In fact, if the opposition force were not there, you would be disappointed that you were not able to show off your skills at the game.

THE CELESTIAL GAME

Somewhere along the line, from our birth until now, we all have been misinformed. Somehow, we gained the impression that the ideal life should be without struggle. Instead, we find that life, at times, just seems plain unbearable. If life is truly terrible, why don't we just check out and tell God, "I no longer want to be your victim. You can play the game without me." For some mysterious reason, we are enchanted by life and cling to it with all our might. Why?

For the greater part of my life, I could not understand the real reason for human existence. It all seemed so pointless. You eat, you go to work or school, then you come home to sleep so that you can repeat the process all over again tomorrow. Eventually, you are old and sick, you cannot eat or sleep very well, then you die. Basically, life is pointless. If the world didn't exist, you and I would all be happier.

WHY CREATION?

Seventeen years ago, I asked a great teacher, "What is the purpose of creation? It seems so random. We try so hard to make a good living so that we can die more comfortably. If that is the case, then why don't we just die now instead of struggling until we become old and sick and more miserable?"

He answered me with the following: "For a moment, let me take your mind back to the beginning of the universe, to the place where it all started. Look, there is One Force. This One has all and lacks nothing, is infinite without limitation, pulsating with great joy, and absorbed in His Own bliss. (author's note: I use He as the pronoun for God realizing full well that God is without gender and/or includes both genders. Read as 'He/She.') Some call This, God.

"However, for no compelling reason—for the sake of pure sport—He multiplies Himself. He multiplies from the One to the many. From the many, the universe comes into existence. As the great Chinese philosopher, Lao Tzu, also said: 'Tao, the Ultimate, gives birth to the One. The One gives birth to two. Two gives birth to three. Three gives birth to the ten thousand things.' From a unified whole He becomes the whole world. He creates a universe full of contradictions. It is a world of the battle between the haves and have-nots. From the One, He creates every aspect and polar opposite of the universe—goodness and evil, intelligence and ignorance, wealth and poverty, success and failure.

"Through the process of creation, He chooses to forget His infinite, all-knowing divine nature and takes upon

Himself the facet of ignorance. He plays the material game of being a limited human being. He is simultaneously eminent and transcendent.

"When the Creative Force takes the forms of human beings, the game then becomes an attempt to regain His divine origin—the original, unified Godself—through the mundane living of life's challenges, the overcoming of self-imposed shortcomings and flaws.

"Humans are made in the image of our Creator. The characteristics of all-pervasiveness, omniscience, omnipotence, complete, unqualified love, and pure, ever-new bliss plus countless other qualities, are secreted within the deep recesses of each of our hearts. Through the game of creation, the Almighty takes on the qualities of ignorance and then struggles to rediscover Her/His Godself.

"If you are made from the substance of that Power, how can you be anything but That? Just as a lion cub raised among sheep is still a lion although he mistakenly thinks himself a sheep, so a human may think they are but a helpless human, yet their God-nature within remains unblemished and ever-blissful. Even the game of struggle, to realize our highest potential in the material and spiritual realms, in our daily lives is nothing but a play manufactured by our Creator and our individual spirit.

"There is no fun if everyone has a basketball on the court, so we create a game where there is only one ball, and we experience the enjoyment of polishing our ball-playing skills. The power of creation caused a contraction of the God consciousness into human consciousness; from the almighty, universal power into the limited, material laws of physics. The game of creation is for the enjoyment of our Creator and, being one and the same, the spirit of humanity. Through tough competition and struggle, we learn the joy of breaking through the self-imposed human limitations and expressing our God-like greatness."

Now that we have covered the concepts of the whole scope of creation, we come back to the original question asked above: "For what mysterious reason are we enchanted by life and cling to it with all of our might?" The short answer is that even as the mind and body are experiencing the drama of human struggle, the spirit considers this devastating struggle part of the fun.

THE STRUGGLE IS REAL

Seventeen years ago, when I heard this statement, it was merely words. Now that I am able to fully experience life as God's playground, I see all is intended for everyone to grow, to expand, to have fun.

Making a bargain with God, the spirit of humanity said, "I want to have a body and be human. As spirit, I am all-pervasive and experience no suffering, no limitations. I am not bound by time, space, or the material world. I am everything. It would be so much fun to be human and pretend to be limited; to have to struggle to obtain, to overcome to obtain, to endure to obtain. Being human is so much fun."

For no other reason than the inborn desire to play, human beings participate in sports. The games may be artificial, but the struggle on the field or court is real. In the pursuit of fun, players are maimed and even killed. However, the best players never lose sight of the reality that it is just a game, after all, and that they have chosen to play in it.

By the same token, you volunteer to play the game of being human in order to enjoy yourself. However, the struggle becomes unbearable when you are caught up in the game, forget who and what you *really* are, and fall out of touch with your divine nature. Forgetting it is just a game, you wander about this earth convinced that you are the victim of God's creation.

The spirit is the spark of that almighty creative power. Within, there are forces that will enable you to achieve anything to which you set your heart. For whether you manifest it or not, the spark of your divine origin remains forever alive within you.

UNDERSTANDING IS NOT ENOUGH

To merely understand the mystery of creation is not enough —it does not help you to make rain, live your life or run your business. The whole purpose of living is tied up with the game of returning to our Godself. The closer we are to our Godself, the more power we acquire to manipulate material reality. The closer we are to our Godself, the more at ease our mind will feel about our business and our life. The more evolved you are spiritually, the more savvy you will be at manipulating the reality of your life and business.

IRRITATION IS A GOOD THING

Agitation and irritation are good things. They are a sign that all things are going well for you. You have taken the first step on the journey to embodying the Rainmaker's secret.

Even if you think you have no desire to be spiritual, whether you like it or not you are a spiritual entity. You cannot help, at some stage in your life, seeking a reality beyond your mundane existence. In most cases this happens when your life starts to whirl out of control. Things are not going well for you on all fronts—in business or your family life.

Stress and irritation are constant elements in your life. As you feel disheartened by harsh reality, you look within to the Almighty for help. Whenever things are not going well, we suddenly become very spiritual.

For most of us, at some time in our lives, we will begin this inner journey. Few are self-motivated through the pure love of humankind and God. We often need a helping hand to push us into embarking on this journey. This helping hand is provided without our permission in the form of the agitation and irritation we feel in our lives.

CONCLUSION

Not until you begin your inner journey can you ever be a proficient rainmaker. (We will speak of this inner journey in detail in the fourth secret of the Rainmaker.) As long as you isolate yourself from the power of universal efficacy, you are only dealing with the limited power of human aspiration. The more you evolve in addressing this universal power, the more you are able to activate the law of synchronicity and hidden coherence.

Our Rainmaker started from this point. It is not because he was so wise that he welcomed the pains of irritable living. Rather, after he lived through the horror of mental irritation, material defeat and spiritual emptiness, he came to realize that the irritation, stress, and overwhelming agitation were merely the first steps toward turning to effortless success—the power which inevitably enhances one's ability to function more fully as a God-child on earth.

SUMMARY

- The human spirit loves games of tough competition. Our life's encounters are identical to our competitions on the sports field. Problems occur when we think that life should be all about how to have it stress-free.

- For no other reason than the inborn desire to play, human beings participate in the games of sports. The players never lose sight of the reality that it is just a game, after all, and that they have chosen to play in it.

- The spirit volunteers to play the game of being human in order to enjoy itself. However, the struggle becomes unbearable when you are caught up in the game, forget who and what you *really* are, and fall out of touch with your divine nature.

- The spirit is the spark of that almighty creative power. Within, there are forces that will enable you to achieve anything to which you set your heart.

- To merely understand the mystery of creation is not enough —it does not help you to joyfully experience life. The key to seeing life as joyous fun is to recreate this mystery in each living moment.

- When the blissful bubbles of joy engulf your heart, even when you are not happy, you are happy.

- Great spirits are often confronted with great challenges in life. Yet, when they are confronted with misfortune, they are able to remain happy in their hearts while they are experiencing these horrific unhappy circumstances.

- Next time when people ask you, "Are you happy?" answer, "Yes, I am always happy, even when I am not happy." Be unlike most people who live life in such a way that even when they are happy, they are unhappy.

- Life is make-believe; life exists in our Maker's dream. The best counsel you can follow is to just keep on dancing to the celestial music, seeing life as a celestial sport. This is the mystical principle that will direct you to operating all of your endeavours from a point of natural harmony.

- Agitation and irritation are good things. They are a sign that all things are going well for you. You have taken the first step on the journey to embodying the Rainmaker's secret.

Secret 2.2:
Grant yourself grace

Life has no exits before the final exit. Once you are on the wagon of life, you are stuck for the full ride; life holds you hostage. The job of a hostage is to figure out how to escape.

STUCK ON THE ROLLER COASTER RIDE

When you are on a thrilling/terrifying roller coaster, whether you enjoy the ride or not, you are momentarily the hostage of the roller coaster ride. This experience of being helpless and frustrated is the same experience as life's overwhelming demands engulfing you. Demands like making a good living, providing for your family, meeting your financial obligations, getting ahead in your job, fighting another battle, winning another war—the list goes on and on. Before you know it, life is not so much fun anymore, you become the hostage of life.

Our Rainmaker knows the secret: the only way you can escape the horror of life is to take refuge in your own mind. Just as on the roller coaster ride, the only choice you have is to choose to enjoy the ride or endure the experience. You have control of how you wish to experience the ride but you are not permitted to stop the ride. A great master once said: "Without the grace of your own mind, even in heaven, you will be without peace." Taking refuge in your own mind, granting yourself grace, is the means to escape the nightmare of unpredictability and fickleness of life.

GRANTING YOURSELF GRACE

We all pray to God at one time or another for His grace in giving us an easy life and having good fortune smile upon us. We also try to be in the good graces of people who have the power to influence others and grant us favours.

When we fall from grace with the 'powerful' and 'influential,' we feel unworthy and devastated by the disapproval. However, have you ever considered granting yourself the grace of your own mind? The *only* reality that exists for you is in your own mind. When your mind showers its grace upon you, the whole world opens up.

STOP THE WHIPPING

Sid, an adviser to the president of a multinational bank, once said to me, "There are three sides to me: In the first state, I am very aggressive, opinionated, and expressive. In the second state, I feel neutral and detached. In the third, I am full of self-doubt, and my mind puts me down. When I am in the last state, I feel like I'm worthless, a pure phony."

From time to time, everyone experiences unworthiness. In fact, when we compare ourselves to our Creator and to our own unlimited, inner potential, we may conclude that we have not turned out so well. Soberly acknowledging that we fall short of our true potential is affirmative evidence that everything is on target. Introspection is a healthy state of mind for personal and professional growth. Letting your mind grab you and use your feelings of unworthiness as a rod to whip you doesn't work.

THE MIND: THE AGENT OF THE SOUL

Countless books have been written throughout the ages on the mystery of the human mind.

According to Western material science, the mind is a phenomenon localized in the chemistry of the physical brain; apart from the brain, mind and consciousness do not exist. However, the Eastern spiritual perception is quite different. The *Yoga Vasishtha* states: "The body has no power to create the mind, but the mind was the driving energy that created the body. The mind is the seed of the body. If the body perishes, the mind can create other bodies." The human brain is a physical organ, but the mind, as the agent of the soul, is a particle of the Divine. An ancient Hindu text, the *Pratyabhijnahridayam*, states that "Universal Consciousness, descending from the Absolute, contracts to become the [human] mind."

Although we experience the location of the mind in the head, ancient Eastern scriptures say that it dwells in each human heart. When the heart is at peace, the mind is calm. When the heart is pulsating with fear and anxiety, the mind is in a state of panic. When your mind showers you with its grace and fills you with delight and harmony, the whole world looks rosy and full of possibilities.

RECASTING FROM HOSTAGE TO FREE MAN

Without the grace of your own mind, even if you are given the grace of the world, you will proceed to sabotage your positive outcome. Some film and music stars, who are thought by the rank-and-file of the world to have everything, end up committing suicide or overdosing on drugs. The mind can be your best friend or worst enemy—creating private heavens or hells.

When Sid, mentioned earlier, is at his low point, he regards his dynamic high points as false illusions. In fact, his high points are more reflective of his spirit nature. The issue is not what is phony or real. Instead, it is that the mind is seeking to identify with a greater force that is the core source of its dynamism. As long as Sid views his achievements as the result of his own effort, his mind will use this fallacy as a pin to puncture his ego's balloon when it is short of air and vitality.

As his unconscious mind knows that he is part of that unique substance of the gigantic force of Creation, it is trying to reveal to him the truth, that he is not the ultimate source of his accomplishments. By practicing the awareness that your power to accomplish is derived from your Maker, you will gain the grace of your mind with every breath taken. You will see life's pace transformed from a struggle to a state of spontaneity. In life's play, you have a choice to recast yourself from a hostage to a free man.

THE ANTIDOTE FOR AN ABUSIVE MIND

You may have the type of mind that drives you to achieve, but no matter how well you do, your mind is never satisfied. Instead of being your friend, it acts like a cruel parent. If you were brought up by abusive or even well-meaning, but exacting, parents, you may experience your mind acting against you just as your parents did, even if they are now absent from your life. Criticize, criticize, criticize. It constantly berates you for never being good enough.

I come from a family that, for generations, has had a history of severe child abuse, that included both emotional and physical punishment. For example, my father's stepmother, during a snowstorm one freezing winter in Manchuria, China, locked my uncle out of the house, forcing him to spend the night huddled in the snow. This act of cruelty caused my uncle to permanently lose his hearing.

On my mother's side of the family, it was not much better. My maternal grandmother, when hitting my mother with heavy wooden blocks, would lock the door of the firewood storage room, anticipating that her neighbour might come to interfere with her unique brand of punishment. One day, concerned that my mother would be killed by my grandmother, the neighbour rode his horse for an hour into town to drag my grandfather out of the local opium den. My grandfather immediately arose from his warm, silken pad that he was occupying with his favourite concubine and forthwith rode home. Upon arriving, he broke down the storage room door and proceeded to savagely beat my grandmother.

In five thousand years of Chinese history, there has been no concept of child abuse. Parents are always right. The Chinese say, "Beating is love, and scorn is tenderness." Under this concept, *anything* the parents can possibly do to the child is said to be for the child's own good. When the physical bruises are long gone, the scars of the emotional damage spill over into every aspect of the child's life after he or she has grown to adulthood.

As I, their firstborn, was a girl, my parents considered themselves cursed from my first day forward. They even blamed me for the Communists taking over in China and for their ensuing loss of wealth. They also blamed me for stealing my brothers' health and wisdom. (One brother was left lame from a case of childhood polio; the other, although a talented artist, is not terribly gifted with life skills and common sense.)

For years after I had left them, my mind behaved just like my parents—whipping me and putting me down. Then I found an antidote that granted me instant freedom. Now, each time my mind criticizes me, I recite, out loud or silently, an acknowledgment of the supreme truism as I have come to know it: "I am perfect and complete. I am the creation of that glorious perfection."

As I repeat this truth with great conviction, instantly I feel a lift that releases the energy of my mind's vicious power. Now, before my mind even begins to start its negative rap, I have learned to repeat this mantra, and my mind calms down. In time, the mind that had acted like a disparaging parent is transformed into a bosom buddy. Now I don't have to repeat this mantra; I really see how wondrous I am. What a shame that my parents can't see it.

For some mysterious reason, we choose a certain set of parents and grow up in a particular environment that is best for our spiritual unfoldment. Your ultimate parents are your Heavenly Father and Divine Mother. Whatever perfection They have, you have. The more you recognize this truth and hold yourself to be perfect, the more you will manifest your perfection.

You don't have to become the victim of your culture, your family's 'well-intended' denunciations, or your own self-criticisms. You are bigger than all of your unfortunate circumstances. Be good to yourself; be sweet to yourself. Don't build a case against yourself. This perfection is living and thriving within you, *as* you.

DROP THE AFFIRMATION, ADOPT THE MANTRAS AND PRAYERS

I would like to draw a distinction here between the use of affirmation and the use of prayers and mantras. When I use the term *mantra*, I want to be clear that I am appropriating a Sanskrit word to define a universal principle, not advocating a certain religion. Whether you call it 'praying without ceasing' or 'practicing the presence of God,' a mantra is not the exclusive right of any specific sect. In fact, although many of us like to feel that we have an edge when it comes to knowing God and His methods, all of the great religions have similar techniques, forms, and truths that mysteriously have been independently sourced by their founders. So your mantra or prayer of choice should come from that particular religious discipline with which you are most comfortable.

Many of our positive-thinking lecturers, past and present, teach the technique of affirmation. Although some have achieved results with these practices, it is my contention that the tool of prayer might be better suited to most temperaments.

The major distinction is that an affirmation may be derived from any source and, because of its origin, may produce a limited or weakened result. The old "Every day, in every way, I am getting better and better" type of affirmation does not have the inherent power for some people to counteract the negative programming that has built up in their minds over a lifetime. Their minds may be self-defeating by answering the affirmation with a sarcastic "Oh, yeah?"—which leaves them spinning their psychic wheels, getting nowhere, and most definitely not becomming "better and better." Mundane affirmations, being born of the earth, are subject to the dualism of the physical world, the mental polarities that cause us so many problems, pulling us in opposing directions.

Prayers or mantras, on the other hand, are of divine origin. Usually, they are a repetition of the divine name, a scriptural phrase, an honoured traditional prayer, or a universal truth. Thus, being born of the divine, mantras are not subject to the dualism of the earthly laws, and they carry within their essence the seed of divine power and truth. This is the real block-busting power that is needed to change lives and circumstances, to move you into the dynamic power vortex that you need to manifest all of your worthy dreams for your life.

When practicing a prayer or mantra, you are not aligning with your limited mental power or success, but with the divine power and truth, which can indeed move mountains.

FIRST GIVE GRACE TO OTHERS, THEN TO YOURSELF

In the beginning of this chapter, I spoke of granting yourself grace and how your mind would set you free. However, granting yourself grace is not easy to do; especially if you customarily hold a nasty attitude towards others. It is impossible for your mind to be nice to you if it has been habitually cruel and vicious toward those who cross your path. How hateful you are towards others will determine how hateful your mind will be to you in equal dosage.

If there is any hope for your mind to grant you grace to recast you as a free person, you need to make every effort to control your hatred towards others. You may not consider yourself a hateful person, but consider whether you burn with rage when people slurp their soup, abort their unborn, marry a gay person, and so on. You may believe with very good reason that they deserve you throwing mental poison darts at them, but a vicious mind is always rooted in a vicious heart. As Lord Buddha said, "When I refuse to take in the abuse from the abuser, then his gift of viciousness will be returned and absorbed by the one who handed out the abuse."

YOUR MIND CAN GROW MONEY

Your mind can create heaven and hell as well as grow money on earth. Recently, an old girlfriend of mine whom I had not seen or talked with for over twenty-five years telephoned me. She said that she had gone through a great deal of trouble to connect with me. She had seen me many times on CNN, on recent interviews with Larry King, and so on. She asked numerous questions about my life to catch up.

Among the many things that I said to her was that I had just returned from working in China for a couple of days. She commented on how lucky I am to be able to travel around the world and be paid for it. She then asked me how much money I had received for a day's work. Because she was a childhood friend I told her. She was silent for a while. Then, with her voice shaking in anger, she said, "I cannot understand what you could possibly do that is worth that kind of money." I did not bother to answer her question because I knew she would not understand.

She demonstrated clearly one of the key reasons why she is not being paid at such a level of compensation. When one considers that a Hong Kong starlet makes one hundred thousand U.S. dollars for an hour of poor singing, and that some Hollywood stars receive eight-figure salaries for working a couple of weeks, we see that our inherent worth is relative to and dependent on the agreement that we have generated for ourselves in the world at large. However, before the world can shower us with our just rewards, we have to experience our own worthiness from within.

Money does not grow on trees—it grows in our minds. How much you should be paid is not controlled by your boss or your customers, it is controlled by you. In the depths of your own mind, where you are really honest with yourself, you have already decided how much you are worth to others. If you think you are worth fifteen dollars an hour, then you cannot have a job that pays five hundred dollars an hour because your mind is incapable of producing that mental picture.

Before you can grow money in the real world, you have to first grow money in your mind. (Just as the Rainmaker made rain in his mind first before he manifested his ability in the physical world.) Others perceive your worth as you broadcast your convictions through nonverbal language, emitting what you truly feel about yourself from every cell in your body. The value that you project to others through your thought processes, consciously or unconsciously, is the value that others will sense to be your true worth.

Furthermore, if you do not know your own value and do not *show* your own value to your client or boss, how can you expect them to decide how much you are worth to them? You have to be clear on exactly what kind of benefits, what kind of real value, you bring to the table.

CONCLUSION

When you are clear about the game of life, that life has no way out and you are life's hostage, you then realize only your mind can save you from the unpredictable horrors of life. Since the human mind is a contracted version of divine consciousness, our minds contain the potential power to create positive and negative experiences and results in every aspect of our lives. Do not frantically keep only the body in motion.

Keep your mind actively dancing on the altar of divine grace as the Rainmaker did. When he first arrived in the village, he closed himself in the tent and meditated for four days, bringing God's grace back into the village. Through focusing the mind on the divine, only then will the force of success gladly do your bidding as you go about the exciting business of unfolding your destiny.

SUMMARY

- The only reality that exists for you is in your own mind. When your mind showers its grace upon you, the whole world opens up.

- The human brain is a physical organ, but the mind, as the agent of the soul, is a particle of the divine consciousness.

- Without the grace of your own mind, even if you are given the grace of the world, you will proceed to sabotage your positive outcome.

- Be good to yourself; be sweet to yourself. Don't build a case against yourself. The universal perfection is living and thriving within you, as you.

- Affirmations, being born of the earth, are subject to the dualism of the physical world, the mental polarities that cause us so many problems, pulling us in opposing directions.

- Mantras and prayers are of divine origin. This is the real block-busting power that is needed to change lives and circumstances, to move you into the dynamic power vortex that you need to manifest all of your worthy dreams for your life.

- When practicing mantras or prayers, you are aligning, not with your limited mental power or success, but with the divine power and truth, which can indeed move mountains.

- Money does not grow on trees—it grows in our minds. How much you should be paid is not controlled by your boss or your customers, it is controlled by you.

- Since the mind is a contracted version of divine consciousness, our minds contain the potential power to create positive and negative results in every aspect of our lives.

- Do not frantically keep only the body in motion. With the techniques of mantra and prayer, keep your mind actively dancing on the altar of divine grace. Only then will the angel of success gladly do your bidding as you go about the exciting business of unfolding your destiny.

Secret 2.3:

Trade what you have for what you want

Faith without works is dead.

— The Bible, James 2:26

Success is not free—you always have to pay for it with the
coin you already have. In order to be a superior rainmaker, our
Rainmaker had to give up being a couch potato watching the
football game or hanging out at the neighbourhood watering-
hole getting smashed. In exchange, he had to contemplate
and study the mystical elements that create drought and learn
how to entice God's grace to shower forth as rain. It was no
small commitment for him to master his professional
rainmaking craft.

LIFE IS ALWAYS FULL

Whenever people think of success, they immediately think of 'more'—more money, more love, more fun and good times, more respect. Yet, upon examination, success is not about having more. It is about what you are willing to give up in order to have what you *really* want.

At any given moment, your life is completely full. Think about it—what was your life like yesterday? You had twenty-four hours, and I guarantee that you used every minute and second of it. You were always doing something—you played, you read, you worked, you fought, you argued, you feared, you worried, you idolized, you breathed, you slept, you ate, you sat, you watched television. Whatever life you had yesterday, it was a full life. You filled every minute of it with something, some activity; even the activity of inactivity.

If you do not like the life that you had yesterday, then you do not do the same things today that you did yesterday. You have to first give up something from yesterday's list to make room for some new, more exciting, reward-oriented activity. Success is not brought about by what you can acquire; it is brought about by giving up something to achieve what you truly want.

A CIRCLE FULL OF STUFF

Imagine a circle in space. This circle is filled with 'stuff', all the stuff that makes up what you call 'your life.' This circle of yours contains all the stuff that you call good or bad tendencies and actions. Whether it is filled with more of one type than the other, the circle is always full. To put anything into this circle, you have to remove some items to make room for your new addition. This is the underlying method and mechanism that success uses to work in our lives.

In order to add success to our circle of business, relationships, or enjoyment, we have to remove something. We have to give up items we like in order to make room for the good that we really want.

PAY FOR YOUR SUCCESS

In order to have enough energy to sustain your demanding workload, you must exchange the pain of exercise for the fun of a television-watching marathon. You must give up those delicious fat and sugary foods for that boring, high-fibre, low-fat diet.

In order to improve yourself and achieve that competitive edge, you have to attend seminars instead of going out with your friends all night to the bars and nightclubs. In order to properly prepare your business proposal and make it a winner, you have to give up your free time on weekends and evenings that you could spend with your family. The list goes on and on.

Lani is a junior college student who dreamed of becoming a professional when she graduated. Deep in her being, she also had a strong psychological desire to become pregnant. I tried to convince her that this was a bad idea, that the responsibility of children at her young age would make it much more difficult for her to get ahead in the world. However, my pleading didn't work. She traded her dreams of early professional success for a child—and a life with a boyfriend who works in a gas station and whom she doesn't really love.

LIFE IS A SUPERMARKET

Picture your life as a giant supermarket, full of desirable things—material, spiritual, and intellectual. However, you cannot purchase anything in this magical supermarket with money. You can only barter with the stuff you already have—your possessions from within your circle.

Try the following mental life-shopping exercise: Go to the market, pick out what you want, and pay for it with what you have. See what you end up with. You should update and reevaluate this list at least once a year throughout your life. Things you thought you truly wanted, you may find you didn't want at all. Things that were not so important suddenly take precedence.

SUCCESS SHOPPING CHECKLIST

List 1—Shopping list: what do I want?

Divide your life into categories, such as career, relationships, family, health, spiritual needs, pleasure, wisdom, knowledge, or any other topics you consider important. In each category, do deep soul-searching, then write out what you really want to have. The sky is no limit for this list, only your imagination.

Example—Sally's Career: I want to be a supermodel with annual earnings of over a million dollars.

List 2—Payment method: how to manifest my desires into reality

The payment method requires taking a sober look at what you have to trade to make room for those new positive results that you want to enter your life. This is a serious how-to process. It is not an unfamiliar process. Each of us goes through this process dozens of times a year when we have to make a decision regarding major purchases.

Consider wanting to buy a Rolls Royce. That's easy—it only becomes difficult when we have to contemplate how we are going to pay for it. Then, obtaining a Rolls Royce becomes very real. Wanting a Rolls Royce and determining how to pay for it are two very different mental states. Depending on our circumstances, this may be trivial or seemingly impossible.

Example: From our case above—Sally wanting to be a supermodel—how can she move from the state of wanting to be a supermodel to actually becoming one? What does she have to give up? In other words, how can she pay for her dream profession with the stuff that she already has for barter in her circle?

1. She will trade in her present eating habits, abandoning all the foods that she loves in order to lose thirty pounds.
2. She will abandon her couch-potato lifestyle in exchange for working with a fitness trainer four times a week, three hours each day.
3. She will budget her cash in order to pay a physical trainer. That leaves her without spare cash on hand for movies and her regular shopping trips with her friends.
4. She will trade her bingo nights in exchange for dance classes. This means she can no longer gossip with her bingo friends about the latest rumours going around the neighbourhood.
5. She will shift other spending priorities. Good skin-care products and a stylish haircut and colouring must now take precedence.
6. She will trade her undemanding but secure secretarial job for an endless series of rejections when she goes to cattle-calls.

7. She will trade in her tender ego for resilience and courage in order to take the endless rejections that come between the few photo-shoots she will be hired for.
8. She will exchange her secure job for a slim chance of maybe or never.

The list goes on. At the end of this effort, Sally will learn where she really stands and what is holding her back from fulfilling her dreams.

List 3—Can I afford it? Do I really want it?

In List 3, rate on a scale from 1 to 10 the difficulties that you will have to go through to exchange success for your familiar behaviour and current way of living. You must ask yourself, "Am I willing to give up my present lifestyle in exchange for having what I really want in business and in life?"

Possibly you will discover that the life you have is exactly the life you absolutely want and that you are unwilling to change a thing about yourself. If so, then you are to be counted among the blessed of humanity. However, know this: if you are *not* content, at least you cannot lie anymore about the idea that life has deprived you of your success.

If you are discontented, but unwilling to give up what is holding you back, you will have to admit that it is *you* who has chosen to reject success and to abandon the dream of being all of the best you can be. If this is so, you can stop getting 'red eyes' whenever you see other people around you succeeding in the life you thought you wanted for yourself.

Remember, you are the captain of your ship. You always have the choice if you are willing to trade what you already have for what you truly want.

Example: After performing the rating exercise, Sally soberly acknowledged that she did not have what it takes to be a supermodel, nor did she really want to be one if it took all that trouble. Sally had to go back to the drawing board to rethink what exactly she was willing to sacrifice to upgrade her life.

GETTING RID OF OLD FRIENDS

As you are climbing the ladder of success, you may find yourself naturally moving away from your old, counterproductive companions and friends. As the cream separates from the milk, so your old friends who do not share your commitment to excellence and achievement can exhibit jealousy and envy as you walk out of their lives.

As the old Chinese saying goes, "When you go near red ink, you become red; when you go near black ink, you become black." To know a person's real nature, look at what kind of people he or she spends time with. Nothing influences you more in your lifestyle, success, behaviour, or habits than the company you keep. People on their way up commonly find that the first things to fall away from them are their non-supportive old friends.

Another Chinese aphorism states: "The wise individual's friendship is as light as the water. The small-minded person's relationship is as sticky and sweet as honey." A true friend is not one who is in your face constantly demanding your attention. They know your life is not about chit-chatting with them; it is about bettering yourself and using your time wisely. In order to be a true friend to you, a person first has to be a true friend to themselves. Friends are self-assured and self-supportive, thus, they can support you while not feeling threatened by your success.

On the other hand, the non-supportive friends are called by the Chinese, "wine and meat friends." They love to party with you, but burn with jealousy whenever they hear joyous news of your career or personal triumphs.

You may discover that many of these so-called friends are really not friends at all. They hate to see you surpass them. In fact, often those friends whom you consider your really, really, really good friends, can be really, really, really jealous of your success. They would much rather see a stranger soar into the sky of accomplishment than see you flying there. They thought you were one of them, so who do you think you are to be worthy of surpassing them? As long you are down at their level with them, they will approve of you. Step out with your accomplishments, and you will have scorn heaped upon your head. Due to their inferior judgments of themselves which keep them bound, they cannot feel happy for you and your advancements. There is nothing you can do to change their minds about you.

You should quietly and graciously walk away. As you clear out your old, jealous companions and useless activities, you are making room for more suitable associations to enter. Let the eagles and dragons enter into your life, and begin soaring among the heights and mountain peaks with them. Leave the old rat pack standing on the low plains of mediocrity.

WELCOME GREATER OPPORTUNITIES

Some of the 'powerful' people who have previously helped you will also drop out of your life. Do not be devastated by their rejection. You will see that it is the will of the Universe for you to move on to a more beneficial environment where you will expose yourself to greater opportunities.

Have you ever noticed that certain 'powerful' people have come into your life at just the right time during different stages of your development? As they have completed their destined journey along your life's path, they naturally drop out to make way for new and more powerful beings to participate with you in making achievements toward your mutual benefit.

ADJUST YOUR ATTITUDE

Tom is a homebody who hates to travel. Ironically, his job requires a great deal of international travelling, as well as sleeping in hotel beds where a thousand strangers have slept before him. Tom hopes that one day the human race will have the technology of instantaneous transportation made famous by the *Star Trek* series—"Beam me up, Scotty"—so that he can go anywhere in the world, take care of business, and return home all within the snap of a finger.

However, since that day may be far off, Tom had to adjust his attitude toward travel. Instead of thinking, as he used to, about how awful it is to travel so much, he now thinks of travelling as downtime that he can spend to clear his mind, be alone, and review his business and personal progress. In a strange town and yet another hotel, he finds that this is a good time to catch up on his relaxation by going to a sauna or having a massage. Now he looks forward to his travel.

Wanting what you don't have or hating what you do have is the fast track to anxiety. Change your mental state from experiencing pain in what you must do, and find within it the experience of fun and adventure. Move your attitude from suffering to joy. A whole world of new experiences will open up for you.

PREPARING TO SUCCEED

Before the angel of success arrives in your life, you should devote yourself to preparing your welcome for her. Polish your craft and strengthen your body to be fit so that you can do your job and enjoy success when it comes. Sharpen your mind and spirit so that they are ready to face the challenges that accompany a visitation from the angel of success.

If you are not ready when the angel knocks, she will flee. And who knows when she will make it back around to your door again? One night in the 1960s, Clint Eastwood and Burt Reynolds were dining together. Clint had already become a famous movie star, but Burt was still struggling, trying to achieve bit parts. Burt asked Clint what he had done before he received his big break. Clint answered that he had simply "prepared myself for success."

Those unadorned words, *preparing for success*, were the advice that was worth ten thousand ounces of gold to Burt Reynolds. He heard the words, understood the profound principle that they held, and went on to stardom.

CONCLUSION

Treat your life as a business venture. Nothing is free. Trade what doesn't work for what you really want. Often, the greater the reward, the larger the adjustments you will have to make in your life. These may include giving up familiar but counterproductive friends, attitudes, and habits.

For our Rainmaker, on the day he was born he did not come with a letter of introduction from Heaven stating, "He is a great rainmaker." It was during the course of his life that he became a superior rainmaker. If our Rainmaker spoke to you now, he would be telling you stories of how he had sacrificed and traded his less productive life for a legendary rainmaking career.

SUMMARY

- Success is not about having more. It is about what you are willing to give up in order to have what you *really* want.

- Your life is a giant supermarket, full of desirable things—material, spiritual, and intellectual. However, you cannot purchase anything in this magical supermarket with money. You can only barter with the stuff you already have—your possessions from within your circle.

- The success shopping list:
  List 1—What do I want?
  List 2—Payment method: How do I manifest my desires into reality?
  List 3—Can I afford it? Do I really want it?

- Nothing influences you more in your lifestyle, success, behaviour, or habits than the company you keep. Let the eagles and dragons enter into your life, and begin soaring among the heights and mountain peaks with them.

- To know a person's real nature, begin by looking at what kind of people he or she spends time with.

- Wanting what you don't have or hating what you do have is the fast track to anxiety. Change your mental state from experiencing pain in what you must do, and find within it the experience of fun and adventure.

- Before the angel of success arrives in your life, you should devote yourself to preparing your welcome for her. Polish your craft and strengthen your body. Sharpen your mind and spirit so that they are ready to face the challenges that accompany a visitation from the angel of success.

Secret 2.4:
Make peace with time

The subject of effortless success would not be complete without speaking of making peace with time. When our Rainmaker arrived at the village, he spent four days in his tent waiting patiently for the moment when God would shower his nectar of rain. He set no deadlines as to when the rain was to fall. He took all of the time needed to bring forth an enormous amount of harmony into himself so it could overflow and saturate the whole village. It took him four days to have the job done. When he started the job, the Rainmaker had no idea how long it would take. There was no mathematical formula that he could use in calculating when the village had enough harmony so the rain could fail. He focused on the job rather than on time.

THE DILEMMA OF TIME

Time existed before you and I, and will be here after we have vanished. Still, to me, time only exists because I exist. Without me, there would be no time. Because I exist, time is here to do battle with me. Time is too short, too long, too boring, too hectic; time flies, time drags; we are late, we are early, we try to buy time, we waste time. We try to manage and control time, but, more often than not, time is in control of us.

Instead of mastering time, we are often mastered by it. Time is like an invisible leech, dominating and victimizing us. We are late for appointments; we are behind in our work; we give up sleep in order to have more time to finish our tasks. We rush here, we rush there, going everywhere, getting nowhere.

Out of desperation, we create the concept of 'time management.' Time management may not work, but as long as we feel we are doing something to manage it, we feel better about ourselves. As far as time is concerned, time never entered into this agreement to be under our management. The *Book of Revelations* (1:8) states: "I am Alpha and Omega, the beginning and the ending, saith the Lord, which is and which was, and which is to come, the Almighty." The ancient Hindu scripture, *Yoga Vasishtha*, says: "Time overpowers everything; time is merciless, inexorable, cruel, greedy, and insatiable."

THE TIME MANAGEMENT GURU HAS NO TIME

At a meeting to discuss turning this book into video and audio sets, a production company executive told me an interesting story:

118

Once they were producing a tape set with Mr X, who is considered the guru on the topic of time management. The production company called Mr X to check if he had rehearsed the script so they could schedule a recording date. Each time they called, Mr X always gave the same answer: "I haven't had time to read it."

TIME—THE UNMANAGEABLE MASTER

Mr X is right, he has no time. In fact his theory of time management which he had marketed so well is an illusion. Consider this: time has existed as long as the creation has existed —billions of years. Time is the witness of history and pre-history and before the concept of history even existed, time was there. How can Mr X, a speck of dust in the vast expanse of the universe with a life span of less than one hundred years, have any power to 'manage' time?

We are not aware that time itself is the master of life, not our work or our 'To do' list. Some people think they know how time works. They hang up their shingles and proclaim themselves to be experts in teaching 'time management.' Yet, anyone who has truly attempted to manage time realizes that it is like trying to manage the universe; it is unmanageable. At best, we come to realize that 'time management' is about managing ourselves, not time. This is the secret that our Rainmaker possessed.

Throughout the ages, mankind has invented instruments —from the hourglass and sundial to the atomic clock—in an attempt to measure, feel, and see time. While humans are busily at war trying to get a grip on time, time stands and ticks away calmly.

An ancient legend tells of an angel in heaven who performed a great ritual sacrifice to the Creator of the Universe. His worship so moved the Creator that He told the angel he could ask for one boon or wish. The angel asked for immortality. The Creator looked troubled. He told the angel this was the one thing that He, the Creator, was unable to grant. "All things," He stated, "will be dissolved in time, even the idea of God and Creation."

THE CHARACTERISTICS OF TIME

Let us consider time—its attributes and aspects. However, bear in mind that this is like trying to bottle the ocean in a single container. Since we know that we cannot bottle time's whole ocean, maybe we can find some key characteristics of time that will allow us to peek into its mystery. Once we know something about time, the question becomes: How can we translate these philosophical, conceptual understandings of time into something useful that will make time our supporter instead of our enemy?

Contemplate and meditate on the hidden meanings of the following points until you can experience them as living realities. You will thereby come to inexorably know that you are the embodiment of time, even as you are a player in the midst of the chaos of daily activities.

- The reality of time exists only within me.

- The reality of time exists within me, without me. It is all pervasive.

- Time is the gift of God. When our time is up, no amount of money can buy us a single extra moment.

- Although time consists of a past and present, with a potential for future, time only truly exists in the moment of 'now.'

- Time is an infinite series of 'nows' strung together.

- Each moment, each 'now,' carries the seed of eternity, and the past and the future.

- The way we spend each 'now' creates our destiny.

- Time does not exist by itself. It exists only within the timelessness of eternity.

- There are two kinds of time: fragmented time and time beyond time.

Fragmented time is the time that most people speak of and experience in their daily lives. This is the experience of time as a cruel taskmaster. Within the framework of fragmented time, there is never enough time; we are always late; we are victims of time.

In the framework of time beyond time, there is always enough time. This is the time of God and nature. In God's time, all things are finished. Even those projects that are not finished are considered so by their not being finished.

In this instance, over-activity is considered an over-rated virtue. God gives us enough time to accomplish all of our honourable tasks. However, our blind ambition directs us to do more and more, telling us more is better until we lose our perspective of God's blueprint for us. We do the wrong things, we correct our wrongdoings, we start all over again. All of the time we are chanting, "I have no time! I have no time!" Managing time is about managing ourselves. It is all about focus, purpose, and priority.

- When we are in the moment of 'now,' we are in timeless-
  ness—the eternity, the time beyond time.

- The experience of the length of time shifts according to our
  state of consciousness. Five minutes may seem to be
  forever, and five hours may seem to be a fleeting moment.

- We experience time differently in sleeping and
  waking states.

  In the waking state, time is experienced in a linear progression. In the sleeping state, time shifts out of order. We
  experience greater freedom. We may be in the 1700s or
  the 2050s and then jump back to the present. During the
  sleeping state, we are closer to the Spirit; thus, time is less
  of a barrier for us to experience than the totality of life.

- The perception of *deja vu* is not a fictional idea—it is an
  experience of reality.

  As a great Chinese master commented on *deja vu* , "All
  this has already happened! As you move close to the
  Truth, you experience it."

- Everything that will happen to us has already happened.

  All things that will happen—our failures, our successes,
  our struggles—have already happened. Like actors who
  have already received their script, we have only to go
  onto the stage and act it out.
  According to Asian wisdom, when we possess an
  unquenchable desire to become an artist, a businessman,
  or a scientist, it is because, prior to our birth, we have
  seen what we will become during this lifetime. Our

success has already been written. We have seen it in the reality that exists in timeless totality, which does not have time's linear dimension.

So, although we don't know *when* our success will happen, we can taste it and feel it and should know that it will happen in its own time frame. Everything we desire will come to fruition in time. If it does not become a reality before our death, we have only ourselves to blame —we have misused time.

- The map of time exists within us.

As we look up into the sky of a dark summer night, we seem to see the sky of now. What we are really seeing is the reflection of time, the shadow of stars and planets that go back in time millions and billions of light-years. Simultaneously, we are looking at different times appearing at once in this present moment.

I was puzzled by the common phenomenon experienced by meditators during deep meditation and by persons just before they fall asleep or awaken, whereby they see a sky full of stars and galaxies behind their closed eyes. The explanation I found opened me up to a view of a cosmology that was greater than any I had ever understood before. As we gaze into our inner galaxy, we are seeing the truth that all times exist within us.

Scientists and philosophers agree that the macrocosm (the infinite, outer universe) exists within the microcosm (the small, infinitesimal universe within each human being). If this is so, then time itself, along with the totality of history, must also be recorded within each one of us. We are the embodiment of time from the beginning of the creation to the end of the final destruction.

- Time is the greatest teacher.

  It accumulates our experiences, both good and bad. In the great furnace of time, we burn up the dross of our ignorance.

- Time is the greatest healer. It heals all pain—all things shall pass in time.

- Time is the greatest destroyer.

  The *Yoga Vasishtha* says, "Imperceptible time, which is beyond even contemplation, devours all and everything! To the lotus of youthfulness, time is the nightfall that forces it to close. To the elephant of life span, time is the lion that brings it down. In this world, there is nothing that time does not destroy. When everything else is destroyed, time itself is still not destroyed."

- Only to those who understand the value of time, all good things will come in time.

- Use time with great respect, and time will reward you.

- A moment of 'now' can transform your life.

  As we have said, time only exists within the moment of 'now.' It can elevate you to the pinnacle of life. When Sharon Stone posed for *Playboy* magazine, in that moment the seed of her destiny for stardom was cast and was but waiting in time to unfold. Yet another moment of 'now' can drop one into the pit of human misery—just as O.J. Simpson's life was forever altered in the moment that Nicole Brown-Simpson was murdered.

- Time is not business as usual.

  Each moment carries the explosive, awesome power to shape and reshape your destiny. Learn to choose your actions well.

- You can touch time and feel time.

  If you ask me to show you what time is, I shall. Stop reading for a moment, close your eyes, listen to that silence that is the sound of time ticking silently within you. Going beyond the silence, feel the Void within you, the bubbling joy of life—that is the feeling of time.

- The more you are in touch with that stillness of time, the calmer and more in control you will feel while you are swimming in the ocean of time's tidal waves.

- Time is the womb of creation and the awesome power of God.

  The nature of time is the nature of God, all good and bliss-filled. Time is not our enemy, not our vicious master. Time and its timeless nature are our very own immortal existence—indestructible, ever-creative, and ever-powerful.

- When you live your life by reacting to the outer chaos, you are at the mercy of time, and time victimizes you.

- When you operate your life from the serene stillness of your inner peace, time protects you and serves you.

MANAGE YOURSELF IN RELATIONSHIP TO USING TIME

Years ago, there was a project that I had procrastinated on for over fourteen months. Finally I had no more time to hide in and had to face it. Miraculously, through my subjective measurement of the amount of work I was accomplishing, it felt like hours had flown by. When I raised my head to look at the clock, I found only five minutes had passed. Since this happened repeatedly, I thought my clock was broken and checked my living room clock—the time was the same. I still could not believe it and found my watch in my purse to make sure all the clocks were correct. This task had caused me agony for over a year. It had taken me a total of three hours to finish it. While I was doing the work, time seemed to just stand still and stare at me.

Out of this experience, I realized time is not fleeting. Even five minutes is a *long* time. It is human ignorance that does not recognize that time is always full of abundance and potentiality. Since then I have not had a similar, dynamic experience about time. However, because I experienced the elasticity of time fully in that single incident, it was enough to bring me to the understanding that I could never lie about not having enough time ever again. I could never again say that twenty-four hours does not provide enough time in a day. Now, when I don't have enough time to finish my work, I know the problem is not time; it is me.

The following tips can provide you with another dimension to look at how to manage yourself in relationship to your utilizing time.

1. Get to know your own characteristics.

How you use your time has everything to do with your personal character traits.

If you are indecisive, foggy-headed, aimless, unclear about your objectives, you may find yourself very busy, working long hours and, yet, accomplishing very little. If you are a deep thinker, you can find that you are very inefficient, ineffective and irritable when you have to do multiple tedious tasks. However, you can create masterful work when you are assigned an extensive task that involves deep concentration. In this situation, time can stand still for you.

If you are action-oriented and physical you will function better with multiple tasks requiring less thinking and more motion. You will find yourself drawn to tasks that allow you to manifest their goals in the real world.

2. Assigning the work.

After understanding what kind of tasks are best suited for you, seek help for, or assign, the work that you don't do well to others. If you are not in a position to give those tasks away, challenge yourself to find the lesson that is there for you in that work. Remember, with the proper approach, you can do anything well.

3. When you are focused, time is under your command.

The common complaint of having no time often comes from allowing everyone around you to steal your time. At work, colleagues stop by your desk to make small talk, unexpected phone calls occur, visitors drop in. It is all about encountering uncontrollable elements that steal your time and make you the victim. The truth is, when you are out of focus first, you subconsciously attract these disturbances. I have watched this principle at work over and over again in my own life.

When I am deeply into writing a book, the Universal Intelligence makes sure I am not terribly disturbed; if the phone rings, I may not answer it so that I do not lose my train of thought. Even if I do answer the phone, the party on the other end (if he or she has any sensitivity at all) can immediately detect that I am deeply involved and they will make it short. Otherwise, I will tell the caller to cut it short or to call back at a better time.

The same thing occurs when I am totally focused on mastering tasks; I also do not idle my time away. Even unexpected visitors or telephone calls do not become obstacles. From my body language and voice they know that I do not wish to be disturbed. To the contrary, when I am totally on purpose, I find that I often attract the specific, beneficial phone calls that tend to help me expedite the completion of my immediate tasks. No joke, it works every time.

4. Just say "No" to others (and to yourself) when you find you are being tempted to deviate from your priorities.

How does one sort out their priorities and decide how to rank them properly? How can we be certain that we are taking care of business and not just spinning our wheels? Nikki Rocco, the president of Universal Pictures Distribution, may have the best definition for maximizing this process in the workplace. She said, "Every day I ask myself, 'What is most important to my division and to the people I report to?' Then I put my priorities in order."

5. Be a detective.

Investigate exactly how you end up frittering your time away. While you do your daily chores, half of your mind should be engaged in performing the work while the other half watches how the time ticks away. Become aware of how much time has evaporated. You might discover that it is not so much that you do not have enough time; rather, it is that you are working without direction instead of charging ahead to complete your task. You move the work from the left side of the desk to the right side of the desk; you are busy but ineffective.

6. Let your dream state do your work for you.

Before retiring for bed, go through your daily task list; what have you accomplished and what will be your priority for tomorrow. While you are sleeping, your subconscious mind will begin to seek the means of accomplishing tomorrow's tasks.

This is not done with any effort that disturbs your sleep. It is an automatic, natural programming. Once your mind receives the direction for tomorrow's purpose, it will simmer and become acquainted with the tasks. By the time morning comes, you will feel that there is a natural familiarity with your 'To do' list. You experience being on top of your day instead of being weighted down by your day. When your competitors wake up and begin to work on *their* 'To do' list after breakfast, they will already be ten hours behind you. You will have gained a ten hour head start.

7. Simplify your tasks.

When you receive a fax, if the answer is very simple and straight forward, just handwrite your reply on it and send it back instead of typing out a new fax.

I once read a report that stated the use of the computer to write letters and faxes takes much more time than writing handwritten notes. It takes time to close the screen you are working in, locate the right directory and files, create a new file name, and type in the name of the fax's recipient. It is so much faster to just handwrite the note, "No problem. It shall be done as per your instruction," or any other simple message. The next time you want to print a letter, send a handwritten note—it is so much more personal and time efficient.

8. Be focused.

Before you pick up the phone, write down the points you want to make and the objectives you want to have accomplished when you hang up the phone. If you can finish a phone call in two minutes, do not take twenty minutes to say the same thing. In another words, don't let others waste your phone time nor should you waste their precious time.

9. Buy more time.

Pay for the most efficient, high-tech tools to accomplish your job. What you are paying for is not new office technology; you are buying yourself more time.

10. Plan less for your day.

Mr Lin of Taiwan's *Success Magazine*, says, "Instead of piling twenty hours of work together into an eight or ten hour day, schedule six hours of work so that you can accomplish it superbly in eight hours. In this way, you will allow time for that unexpected interference. Also always remember, because we live in the physical realm, everything takes longer to do than you think."

11. Play longer hours.

To me, work is the highest play, so I don't mind playing a little longer. The more I play, the more I earn.

12. Disappear the papers.

Lawrence T. Wong is the president of the Hong Kong Jockey Club (the territory's largest taxpayer) and the past president of the Ford Motor Company of Taiwan, the most profitable foreign venture in Taiwan. He imparted to me his secret of eliminating the overwhelm caused by an overflow of paper-work. He stated, "You should never touch the same paper twice. Once you have touched it, there are three things you must do with a given piece of paper: handle it, file it, or throw it away.

For those papers that are just screaming "keep me, keep me" and don't want to be thrown away, Larry Wong also has a method:

1. Create three drawers: A, B, C
   A-Relatively important
   B-Less important
   C-Least important

2. Every 7-10 days, throw away all the paper in the drawer C.

3. Then, demote drawer B to C and drawer A to B. In time, all the papers will be handled without ever having to handle them.

When asked how he came up with this method, he told the following story:

He once worked for a boss who kept mountainous piles of paper on his desk. Curious as to what his boss's reaction might be, he hid one pile of his papers in the closet for a month. His boss never missed them. He then brought those papers back and hid another pile. His boss again did not realize anything had changed. His conclusion was that his boss had been using his desk as an archive filing cabinet.

Many of us are also using our desks as storage instead of using the filing cabinet. By doing this we create chaos for our minds. We are sending our mind the subconscious message that we have more to do than we actually do. Our mind becomes agitated by the overwhelming volume of the paper on our desks and, consequently, is not sharp and precisely focused on the immediate task that is before it.

The answer—clean it up!

13. Antidote for a mild case of ADD (Attention Deficient Disorder).

Occasional ADD is a common condition to which many of us are prone. It is usually created by interaction with our overly demanding world. For those who have never experienced it, you cannot imagine how irritating it can be when it occurs.

On one occasion, for example, I noticed that I had walked into my bathroom but, upon arriving, had forgotten why I had gone there. I stood in front of the mirror and asked myself, "Why am I here?" Eventually, I remembered that my original purpose was to wash my face.

To cure this situation, you must mentally verbalize your initial thought (wash face, get coffee, etc.) before and during your excursion. If you have these mild ADD tendencies and don't do this, the chances are good that by the time you arrive at your destination you will have had at least ten more unconscious thoughts that will have crowded out your original impulse to action.

So, the remedy is to follow this sequence of events:

1. A thought triggers your initial desire for action, such as washing your face.
2. Say it silently or softly to yourself, "washing face."
3. Follow the command by walking to your destination. Verbalize softly your intention while walking to your destination.

If you think this is too much work, it is not compared to the reward. Practicing this technique will evolve your mind toward being less foggy, and becoming more clear with repetition. You will see a dramatic change in your relationship with time.

If you ever find yourself saying, "I don't know where the time goes," you are a candidate for this exercise.

Incidently, after I had written this section, my editor told me about the technique that the Buddhist monks use to 'stay in the present.' Whatever action they are performing, they repeat the word as a mental mantra to remind their minds not to drift off in idle rumination. So, while they are walking, they will mentally say, "Walking, walking."; while eating, they repeat, "Eating, eating."

14. Planning your time backwards.

It is so much easier planning your time backwards rather than looking forwards. Take your project deadlines and work them backwards, so that you can realistically project when you must start your tasks and determine by when, what has to be accomplished.

For example, if I'm going to catch a flight departing San Francisco International Airport at 9 am, then, obviously, I need to be at the airport at 8 am to accomplish all the preliminaries involved. It takes an hour and a half to travel from my home to the airport.

Also, I must remember to allow for a possible traffic jam (they happen often), so, I need to leave my house two hours before 8 am. I know it will take me one hour to be ready to leave the house and, lastly, I add 30 minutes for unexpected problems (missing keys, last minute phone calls from the East coast, etc.). This means I must be up at least by 4:30 am to leave the house at 6 am to arrive at the airport by 8 am in order to catch the 9 am flight. No stress; everything is under control.

15. Always over-estimate the time needed to complete your project.

People tend to underestimate the time needed to complete a task. In the depths of our being we are mental and spiritual beings; when we look into the future to estimate the time needed for a task, we look subconsciously from the spiritual and mental realms, and from that vantage point, the task always seems easier. Years ago, I wanted to build a 'romantic' stone house on my Oregon mountain property. I bought a guide book that stated how easy it was to build a stone house with your own, two little hands. In my mind it was a piece of cake. I could just see that little ginger bread house standing in the midst of the green forest . When I started to struggle with the real stones and cement, reality set in.

To get it right, you may want to over-estimate your project time by a minimum of three times longer; some projects realistically may take five to ten times longer. This is all according to how real you had set your initial estimate. Consider those professional estimators in civil projects, movie budgets, product development, and how they are almost always into time and cost overruns.

Sean owned a custom software engineering company. In order to sweeten the deal, he often underbid the time for delivery. After the due date came and went, while the software was still in shambles, the client would start to complain. A two-month job would eventually be finished in ten months. During the eight months schedule extension, he was in hell. All of his energy focused on how to calm the rage-filled client. Often he would have four or five livid clients at the same time.

Eventually Sean lost his business. He had spent so much energy focusing on putting out the fires that it left him with no time to generate new business. Even if he received a potential new client interested in his service, his existing clients would sabotage him by pouring out their upsets when it came time for references.

Sean should have had the courage to estimate realistic times needed to deliver a project. However, he was driven by the fear of losing jobs, so he won't tell the truth.

16. Focus on the job, not the time.

When a project becomes violently driven by time, stress and fear set in as job integrity goes out the window and disaster waits to happen. On 28 January, 1986, when the Kennedy Space Center launched the tenth space shuttle flight, it blew up like a giant fire cracker on television and killed all of the eight astronauts on board. My first intuitive thought was that this horrible event had been caused by preventable human error; that someone in charge of the project had been driven by fear of an overrun in the budget or missed deadlines. A year later, the cause of the disaster was disclosed and it proved my instincts to be correct.

NASA had gone ahead though the shuttle was not ready to launch; even though a senior engineer protested that the o-rings had problems. This resulted in the most regrettable and tragic space accident ever. How can you replace the lives of those precious human beings on board? The tragedy was caused by the person in charge having his eyes on the time, not on the job.

17. In God's time, all things that should be done, will be done.

In our modern world, doing more within less time is a great virtue. However, more of the 'wrong' thing should not be considered as virtue at all. Sometimes it can be downright deadly. The KLM and Pan Am Airlines jets that collided on the airport runway about a decade ago caused one thousand deaths. It was consequently found to be the KLM pilot's eagerness to take off so he could make up for lost time—over the judgement of his co-pilot. If the KLM pilot had any under-standing of how to make peace with time, a thousand lives, including his own, could have been spared.

18. You don't have to do it all.

For the little or the much that you have accomplished today, congratulate yourself. Whatever you did not finish, so be it. If you died right now, you would not miss all your unfin-ished tasks.

CONCLUSION

Peace of mind comes from understanding the object that you are dealing with. The understanding of time is vital to your success without stress. Without time on your side, there will be no peace of mind and joy of life. You exist in the timeless-ness of eternity. Take refuge in time: stop managing it, make peace with it. Making peace with time translates into making peace with yourself. Focus on the job, not the time.

When you are at peace with yourself, then your life, your work, your commitments, your schedules, your 'To do' list, and your ambitions will be supported by the synchronicity and hidden coherence of your life that, in turn, gives life to time. For those who are at peace with time, as our Rainmaker is, success is but a small reward.

3rd Secret:
Find the resting point within

When the Rainmaker disappeared into his tent for four days to put himself in harmony, he didn't just go to sleep for four days. Sleep is not a true resting point for the mind and soul. While you sleep your body tosses and turns, your mind is actively creating fantasies and nightmares. Only by finding the true resting point within, will your body, mind and spirit be truly restful.

Like the pendulum of a clock that has ceased its wild oscillations, in every situation there is a relaxation point where all things simply settle in comfortably. This is the point where harmony, excellence, beauty, and synchronicity abide.

Release the mind from its frenetic irritation caused by the constant stimulation of the senses. These sense stimulations are activated by the mind striving after its desired objects. As long as the mind is focused on fulfilling its 'ever new' desires, it remains in an eternal state of exasperation. When we cut the cord of sensory desires by pulling the awareness from its involvement outward to its focusing within, then we will find this magnificent point of true satisfaction.

Just rest yourself in yourself. I do realize, though, that sometimes the simplest things to say are the hardest things to do. The rest of this section will explore exactly how one goes about doing precisely this.

Secret 3.1:

From reacting to restfully controlling

Imagine our Rainmaker first arriving at the village. The villagers have not seen a drop of rain for five years. Yet, during the five years, they have seen rainmakers come and go, money spent and money wasted on the employment of rainmakers. Hopes are raised and then dashed with each new rainmaker's broken promises. When our Rainmaker arrives at the village he must shield himself from reacting to the emotions of the villagers. Otherwise, he would have no hope of bringing a single ounce of harmony to himself, not to speak of the whole village.

When you drive on the freeway, you learn to react to the traffic situation. In the workplace, when people attack you, you learn to react to protect yourself. In your business dealings, at the negotiating table, you react to the cards that are dealt to you. You react to your husband's or wife's aggression. Through the instinct of survival, reacting to your environment has become second nature to you.

Reactionary people are always controlled by the person or element that imposes the impetus to action upon them. When you operate out of reaction, you lose control. You have been swept from your power centre. Reacting causes you to appear to be weak. Worst of all, you *feel* weak. As long as you are reacting, you have lost sight of your own agenda.

The following methods are ways to move yourself from reacting to restfully controlling:

1. Be the actor and the director.

Instead of functioning by acting and reacting, with your reaction always one step behind the person who is imposing his or her will upon you, imagine splitting yourself into two halves. One part of you becomes the actor performing the action, going through your usual ten thousand daily items, while the other part of you is the director resting inside your heart, watching your actions and the activities around you. Unlike your competitors, who are operating out of acting and reacting, you will now have the edge—a team of two at work: the one who is performing the action, and the other who is witnessing and directing. You have both an actor and a director.

The director, sitting inside you, sees the curve ball coming long before you, the actor, do. The director then decides whether you should step to the side at the last minute and let the ball pass you by or take a head-on strike. Either way, you are not blindly reacting to the situation, which will rob you of your sense of power and jeopardize your good judgment.

2. Replenish your power and serenity.

To be continuously reacting to life will cause spiritual and emotional depletion. No matter how you reason with yourself that you should not be stressed or overwhelmed by life, it does not work if you are mentally and emotionally overdrawn and spiritually bankrupt. Your life energy works the same way as your bank account. You cannot keep withdrawing from your pool of serenity without making periodic deposits. You need to make a deposit of the nectar of life into your spirit before you can extract from the pool of enthusiasm. In the centre of your heart is a pool of serenity where power, wisdom, passion, and the zeal for life renew themselves.

3. Redo the scene.

If you find that you have over-reacted to a mole-hill-size situation with a volcanic, explosive psychic outburst, when you calm down, do an instant replay in your mind's eye while properly adjusting your reaction. Then, re-do the scene again with these adjustments in mind. By repeating this process over and over again, you will learn to correct your tendency to overreact.

4. Resting within.

Resting within is much simpler than most people think. It is the innate nature of our being. It is about resting in the heart. When you feel frustrated about life, when it does not instant-aneously manifest your desires, instead of going through a frantic reaction, go within and take a rest in your heart. Resting within provides you with all the benefits that you normally derive from meditation, such as reducing your stress and calming your mind. Furthermore, practicing resting within will gradually transform your business encounters from a state of 'reacting' to one of 'restfully controlling.'

In secret 3.2 we will explore extensively how we can find that resting point inside of us.

CONCLUSION

If you want to leap from 'reaction' to 'restfully directing' your life, go within and rest in the heart, take a dip in the pool of peace, replenish yourself. If you continuously make withdrawals, you should intermittently go into the vault of your heart to make deposits. While the actor is performing on the world stage, the director should be resting in the calm pool of the heart. Our Rainmaker knows the secret art of restfully directing his life and his environment rather than blindly reacting to the chaos that surrounds him.

Secret 3.2:

Find the resting point

As competition becomes fiercer, surface data and simple logic are no longer sufficient as the only source of information to help executives in making complex decisions. They must go beyond the obvious, bypassing the tunnel-vision of standard planning processes, to find bold new solutions. They, of necessity, must reach for the new frontiers of the realities beyond the normal.

EFFECTIVE BUSINESS TOOLS FOR THE TWENTY-FIRST CENTURY

The leading European business school, INSEAD (located in the suburbs of Paris), has concluded from its research that the two most effective new business tools for twenty-first century executives are *meditation* and *intuition*. The same conclusion was reached at the Harvard Business School.

Mr Claude Rameau, the Dean of INSEAD (honoured as the Dean of the World), told me, "We do not know how to teach meditation and intuition, so we built a large meditation hall for teachers, executives, and students to just sit quietly and contemplate resting within." However, what is the so-called 'new' is actually the old and ancient.

Meditation, the science of internal access, allows you to discover wisdom and information that you do not know you have. This is the state of natural knowing, commonly referred to as intuition. All the things that I do well in life I have acquired by tapping into the channels of natural knowing. The knowledge and wisdom mysteriously spring up from 'nowhere.'

Through meditation, you will discover a fountain of creativity, the outrageous intuition that resides within you. Through meditation, you will become in touch with your power; you will become intuitive and creative naturally.

FINDING THE RESTING POINT

As we said earlier, when the Rainmaker disappeared into his tent, he didn't just go to sleep because even sleeping is not a resting point. Only by finding the resting point within can our body, mind and spirit truly rest.

The following techniques allow the activity-oriented mind to rest in the calming space of the heart. These techniques have been proven by the ancient teachers to be highly potent. I have selected the following methods because of their practical nature; they fit into today's hectic business lifestyle. These techniques are simple to practice and will make a profound difference to your daily life.

Merely understanding the words of the following techniques is useless to you. To derive any benefit, you must routinely put the techniques into practice, and that is easier said than done. Like a soldier of the Revolutionary War, understanding how to load the gun powder into the firing arm will not save your life. Only through repeated practice, until your actions move to the level of reflex and become ingrained habit, can you become ready to face life's battles and win.

1. Being in the presence of silence.

This is the simplest way to rest in the heart—to be in solitude and to bathe in the joy of silence. Silence is the veil of God. Take time for a long luxurious bath and lock out the chaos of the world. Take a walk in the woods. There are infinite ways you can be with silence. In the centre of that silence is the seat of that inner resting point.

2. Focus on a single idea or object.

When the mind is vacillating, moving from one thought to another, the mind is agitated. When the mind is absorbed on one single idea or object, the mind is at ease with itself. People who play golf know this well. When the player is on the course, their focus is on that white ball. They are bewitched by that white ball. The golfers may tell their office or their spouse that they play golf because it is a good opportunity for business networking when, in fact, they are addicted to the joy they experience when their mind is focused deeply on one single object. So they follow the ball to the hazard or to the tree top.

For the non-golfer, taking a hot bath will give you the same experience. Close the door; lock out all of the chaos of the world. Immerse yourself in the steaming hot water. Focus your mind on letting go and empty your mind of thoughts. We often think it is the hot water that is so enjoyable. In fact, it is the act of letting go that is the comfort source for the mind. Just imagine if, while you were inside the tub, five telephone lines were ringing, demanding your attention, would you feel restful?

3. Contemplating open space.

Verse 85 of the *Vijnanabhairava* says: "You should contemplate vast open space, such as the sky or ocean, and see them as the essence of God, letting that feeling dissolve within you. Through this inner expansion, you will be absorbed and see everything within the universe as the scintillating light of the divine."

This is the same as the Western idea of finding time to stop and smell flowers. It is not that the smelling of flowers has any special meaning. Rather, when you are performing the act of smelling the flowers, you are experiencing the essence of God, which expresses Itself as the fragrance. You then have the opportunity to let the scent dissolve within you. As it touches you within, you expand inwardly and experience the whole universe as the divine creation of our Maker. Your inner vision opens up to reveal that all things in creation are bathing in the eternal light of the divine.

The experience derived from looking into vast open spaces cradles your restless senses by the calming wellspring of the heart. This is a natural meditation. No wonder people are willing to pay premium prices for real estate with an ocean or mountain view.

4. Bastrika—the breathing exercise.

Breathing is closely connected to the well-being of the mind (not to mention the life of the body). When you regulate your breath, you eradicate agitation from your mind. The reason that most ordinary human beings function from a space of reacting instead of controlling, regardless of their social position, is that the agitation of the mind prevents it from going within to rest on the bosom of God in the human heart.

This rapid breathing exercise is known as *bastrika* in Sanskrit. When one is practicing *bastrika*, he or she may appear to be having a hyperventilation attack. Yet, the mystery contained therein is way beyond the scene that meets the eye.

a. Where: You can do this exercise anywhere, in the midst of chaos or serenity.

b. When: Whenever you feel stressful, restless, or fearful—or if you just want to focus your mind and your spirit. You can practice this exercise before an important meeting or presentation. When you become very skillful at this, you can even do it in the middle of a meeting, and no one will notice.

c. How: Sit on a straight-backed chair that can comfortably support you, or sit on the floor in a cross-legged position. When you become adept at this, you can even do it while you are standing or lying down. (I caution you against doing it while driving or operating machinery since the results can sometimes be exhilarating enough to cause the sensation of dizziness.)

- Take a deep breath and let the breath flow into the bottom of your stomach while you focus your attention on the space between your navel and your pubic bone.

149

- Exhale completely, then *rapidly* inhale and exhale twelve times through your nose, drawing your breath into the lower part of your stomach. This will cause your stomach to rise and fall like a bellows—breathe in, breathe out, breathe in, breathe out. The only part of your body that is moving is your stomach. Your shoulders remain still.

- A set of *bastrika* consists of ten to twelve rapid breaths. This can be modified to a greater or lesser count to a set, depending on the practitioner. You can do as many sets as you want. In general, four or five sets are sufficient. If you are on a bus or a train, you can do fewer sets.

- Don't try to control your breath. The objective is to let your breath express itself freely. You may find that your exhalation is very forceful and long. You may find that, instead of you breathing, your breath is breathing itself. That is, your breathing has become involuntary. I do not mean out of control; rather, your mind is not currently directing your breath—it is directing itself. When you feel that you have had enough, your mind will have the power to stop at any time.

- Doing this breathing exercise will also provide you with instant rejuvenation. This is a great exercise to pick up your energy during the day. This is also a great exercise to prepare you for entering into a deep meditation.

5. The *Ham'sa* technique.

The holy men of all religions have practiced the art of breathing and breath regulation and, through these sacred techniques, have reached into the depths of their souls and the centre of their hearts. In ancient times, the secret of this technique was well guarded. Students had to clean cowsheds for eighteen years to prove their worthiness to receive this profound teaching. I have already described the *Ham'sa* technique in *Thick Face, Black Heart*, but it is so potent that it is worthy of being mentioned again.

In Book Two of the *Essene Gospel of Peace*, Jesus said: "We worship the Holy Breath, which is placed higher than all the other things created. For lo, the eternal and sovereign luminous space, where rule the unnumbered stars, is the air we breathe in and the air we breathe out. And in the moment betwixt the breathing in and breathing out is hidden all the mysteries of the Infinite Garden."

Verse 24 of the *Vijnanabhairava* says something very similar: "The exhalation goes out, and the inhalation goes in. By steady fixation of the mind at the two spaces between the breaths, one may experience the full nature of *Bhairava*—God."

The following are the steps of this ancient meditation technique. However, even if you don't follow the steps and just sit for a while and watch your breath, all will be well.

- Select a serene place in your home, preferably a room dedicated for prayer and meditation. If that's not possible, assign a corner to be used for this purpose only.

- Wear loose clothing of natural fabrics—silk is preferred. Meditators from ancient times to the present have experienced that silk clothing elevates your meditative experience. The explanation by some, though not scientifically provable, is that silk insulates you from the mundane, earthly vibrations. Putting it simply, you may experience a better meditation while you are wearing silk clothing.

- Wearing the same set of clothing during meditation is preferred. You should keep the clothes very clean so you

151

do not have to wash them often. The reason that you should have a regular place and regular clothes for meditation is to accumulate the meditation energy in one place within one set of clothes. Doing this will help you to quickly enter into the high state of meditation.

- Establish an altar—a place to put the image of your saviour or chosen deity to inspire your devotion.

- A candle or fragrance can also be used to create a serene mood. It is advisable to select the same fragrance each time, so you associate the fragrance with your meditation.

- Sit quietly on a wool mat or on a chair covered with a wool mat, with your back relaxed but erect. The use of a wool mat is recommended for the same reason that I suggest wearing silk clothing. The wool mat also acts as insulation. It has been stated that a wool mat can become saturated with positive energy accumulated during your meditation, and thus help you to more quickly and easily enter into a state of deep meditation.

- Close your eyes. Bring your attention to your breath.

- Watch your breath naturally go in and out of your body.

- Listen to the sound of your breath. As you breathe in, your breath makes the natural sound of *ham*, and as you breathe out, it makes the sound of *sa. Ham* in Sanskrit means 'I am,' *Sa* means 'That'—Spirit. Humans breathe 21,600 times a day, and each time the breath repeats *Ham'sa*, trying to remind us of our divine heritage. I am That which created me. You may think the syllables as you breathe without uttering them out loud.

- Listen to your breath silently as you breathe in and out, watching the space between the inhalation and exhalation. Observe the space where inhalation meets exhalation. Behold the space between the breaths, for it is the gate to the mystery of this Universe and beyond.

- Sit for five minutes to half an hour or longer, as you see fit.

6. The non-meditator's meditation.

The experience of resting within is also available to the non-meditator because, in a broad sense, life is one gigantic, continuous meditation process. The beatific experiences gleaned from meditation is also available in our daily lives. The soldier in the midst of battle knows that, even while experiencing acute fear, he feels sometimes an exhilaration at the same time —an overwhelming experience of being alive fills them while in the very jaws of death. While looking into the eyes of fear, the soldier sees God's primal power. The same may occur after a fit of rage. Our minds can become unusually tranquil because within the centre of such strong emotions lies the raw, potent power of the universe.

Even without being in a place of worship or meditation, by simply gazing into the vast, open spaces of the desert, ocean, or sky, we can experience a miraculous ecstasy bubbling up from within us. Playing golf is a form of walking meditation. Relaxing in a rocking chair and gardening are ways that lead you to rest in the heart.

However, it is simply easier and more dependable to consciously and steadfastly travel through this wondrous territory using the directed means of prayer and meditation than to occasionally hit upon spontaneous transcendental experiences.

CONCLUSION

Our Rainmaker has the unique ability to rest within himself so deeply that he can bring the grace of God to the village out of synch with the Divine. He is a regular, committed practitioner of meditation. As the Chinese saying goes: "If you don't engage in meditation daily, when you are in need of the Buddha's help and attempt to grab onto the Buddha's feet, it won't work."

4th Secret:
Let spirituality energize business

In order to discover the business skill of the Rainmaker, we do not speak of business, but rather focus on spiritual matters. As I have said in my books, "There is no division between the business strategies of getting ahead and spiritual evolution." The more evolved spiritually one is, the more savvy they will be in mastering a life that includes business.

Our Rainmaker's job is to make rain. When the rains come, it means a job well done. If the rain does not come, he is castigated for failing to make rain. His job results are measurable in material reality. Nonetheless, behind the material reality is hidden the real story of how the Rainmaker 'negotiates' with the spirit world to bring rain upon the earth.

The closer you are to the spiritual realm, the more you will excel in your professional achievement. I cannot repeat myself often enough about the validity of this dynamic verity. Excellence in business on the surface is about the ability to manipulate material reality, yet in truth, business is beyond reality; it is also magical.

Knowing these mystical concepts brings comfort to our minds when we come to see that this material universe is a mirror and the reflection of its Maker; that behind each 'mundane' pursuit in our lives there lies the power hidden in the great mystery of God's miracles. Through the events in our lives and the marvel of nature's silent unfolding, God reveals His power. It is to our benefit to uncover God's power and let the power of spirit energize our business encounters. Without borrowing the power of God, how could our Rainmaker make rain?

To merely understand the mystery of spiritual matters is not enough, it does not help you in making rain or achieving success in your life and business. The inner journey of life is a game of returning to our Godself. The closer we are to our divine centre, the more power we acquire to manipulate the material reality. The closer we go, the more at ease our minds become about our business and our life.

As we are spiritual beings made in the image of our Creator, our success is not solely dependent upon our performance in the material realm. Our success is also greatly determined by our ability to employ the full spectrum of subtle elements of the mental and spiritual realms. The spirit is the spark of that almighty creative power. Within you, there are forces that will enable you to achieve anything you set your heart to. For whether you manifest it or not, the spark of your divine origin remains forever alive.

Secret 4.1:
The spiritual power of the Rainmaker

That which thy fathers have
bequeathed to thee, earn it anew
if thou wouldst possess it.

— Goethe, Faust

Our Rainmaker, in four days, was able to generate such harmony that it could flow out of his being into the whole village. His action was powerful enough to neutralize the disharmony in the heart of every villager and bring relief to their five years of drought. This Rainmaker's power was not the work of a neophyte.

In this chapter we will examine the inward journey that the Rainmaker travelled prior to his arrival at the village, the journey that had provided him with the intelligence to recognize the source of the drought, the solution to the problem, and the ability to manifest the desired results as his 'business' objective. Most importantly, you may be asking, what does all this have to do with us who live in New York, Tokyo, Paris or Sydney? How does studying the Rainmaker's spiritual journey affect our day-to-day life and business?

ALL PATHS LEAD TO ONE

Our Rainmaker, like all people on the path of life, had to walk through the seven stages of the cleansing process which we will explore in depth in this chapter. From the Christian Bible in the Book of The Revelation by the Apostle Saint John to the ancient scriptures of the East, from the Moslem Sufis to the Jewish Kabalah, all speak of the seven seals or the seven levels or centres of knowledge. Even Mozart, in his opera The Magic Flute, told of a journey through the seven rings of knowledge as a process of self-purification, a dropping of the burdens of man's ignorance, a gaining of a piece of God's power.

Coincidentally, from the ancient to present, East to West, independently, all of the great spiritual leaders have discovered and recorded the secrets of the seven levels. This is the inner blueprint of the interior journey that our Creator has hidden within us to allow us travel unto our divine destiny. Those who have experienced what I speak of, know the reality of these definitions; those who have not, if they are willing to observe and experience, will soon come to know what I say is so.

THE THREE PERSPECTIVES

I look at this dynamic enigma from three different perspectives, the Eastern perspective, the Western perspective, and the human perspective, to let you see that people from all walks of life reap the same spiritual and worldly benefits from their particular journey and thus share a very similar phenomena.

The Eastern perspective focuses on Eastern philosophical points. The Western perspective is taken from the traditional Christian viewpoint. If you are from the West and relate to the Western reference point, you may find the Eastern perspective to be somewhat odd and, yet, you may find it exciting to learn how the East looks at the same truth. East and West have no division in the eyes of our Creator; the division only exists to human eyes. Christians, Hindus, Buddhists, Moslems, and Taoists simply use different reference points to speak of one common experience of the universe.

The human perspective is included to address the relevant points from the practical day-to-day reality of survival because the mystery of life is not solely designed for the benefit of meditators. Spiritual matters are also relevant to non-spiritually minded people because life itself is meditation and is the one, huge meditation process that we all participate in. When people give an effort by practicing meditation, they accelerate the process of the journey through the seven stages. For the non-meditator, the seven stages are equally available, just a little slower, because the mystery of life and spirit is imbedded in the process of life itself. The reason you even take birth is to learn about the deeper meanings of life. Throughout life, you learn about the wisdom beyond life. Even for people who think they are atheists, I guarantee you that they know something of God, although they may not call that force the Divine. Whether you are spiritual or not, you cannot avoid the journey through the seven stages.

If anything is true, it is that every culture has had the same experience of the one truth. It cannot be only good for the Christian, but not right for the Buddhist, Hindu, or Jew. That which is true will touch the religious as well as the non-religious person,even if they can only understand life through the experience of living it.

Once Picasso told Claude Monet, "We are not religious."

Monet replied: "Yes we are. When we paint, we are doing our worship and meditation."

THE SOUL'S INWARD JOURNEY

Writing about the seven stages is a very difficult task, but I find that it is most necessary because too many spiritual teachers have misinformed the neophyte that when one incorporates spirituality in their life, harmony and angelic peace will ensue; not true. Often the spiritual seeker, in the beginning, does not see themselves becoming better; it seems only worse, and find that they are becoming unbelievably difficult to live with. This has caused untold amounts of grief.

One common occurrence is that you do not become calmer and sweeter as you thought you would, but rather, you become really irritated. This excessive irritation, as we have mentioned in an earlier chapter, is not only caused by outside stimuli; it also results from inner unfoldment because we have all accumulated certain characteristic negative tendencies.

If you believe in reincarnation, it is what is called the karmic impressions. All of these negativities must come out to be expelled. This irritation is just one of the characteristic tendencies that we have stored within us. I have mentioned in the earlier chapter that irritation is a good thing because it is connected to the process of our spiritual evolution. The opening up of the first three stages will cause you to feel intense irritation. I could not explain it deeper until now.

If, at any stage, you are having difficult experiences, understanding the nature of the seven stages will help you realize that there is not something inherently or permanently wrong with you. Rather, this is a natural phenomenon, and a great amount of people from the East and the West have had similar experiences.

The seven stages of unfolding are an exciting journey that can also be very confusing. If one experiences the process of unfolding without a road map to the knowledge, the confusion can be exacerbated by agony, doubts and fear. By having a road map, you will know that you are on the right track and you can enjoy the wonder of these manifestations. Although the journey is as precarious as walking on the razor's edge, it is also full of rapture, ecstasy, and wonder.

Each day you discover something new about yourself. You are not the same person today as you were yesterday. Although your friends think they know you, you realize they don't have a clue about what is happening within you. At times you may have three years of mental growth condensed into the short span of one day.

The greatest pain is growing pains; the greatest joy is also the joys of growth. Without undertaking this inner journey, there is no aliveness. Ninety percent of our inner power usually lies dormant. Being ignorantly blissful is no bliss at all. The mental-spiritual state of true happiness cannot be understood through logic; it can only be known through direct experience. Only when you have made the journey will you know the truth contained within these words and the inadequacy of these words to convey the essence of the seven stages of unfolding.

UNCOVER YOUR INNATE TALENTS

The seven stages of spiritual unfolding, directly affects the unfolding of one's ability to manifest physical innate talents for mastering attainment in the material world. This is why certain people, during their adulthood, uncover extraordinary talents that they did not know they possessed. By following their newly discovered talent, they fulfill the promise of destiny.

TO BEGIN

What I am about to reveal is not suited to all readers. Some may find this information is not for you at this stage of your life. For those, close the book now! Whatever you have learned to this point is more than enough to feast on for a lifetime. You may open the book unexpectedly on a misty morning sometime in the future and say, "This is it...Everything I ever wanted is right here in this chapter."

The notion of the seven stages of the inner spiritual journey is not the property of any particular religious practice or sect. It is a documented, universal experience and phenomenon, belonging to all and denied to none. No one can hide from its power. The power that propels this process is rooted in life itself.

The information from here on is not to be read only. You should take a small passage and contemplate upon it. The information is not to be understood by the mind. Unless you practice prayer, meditation and devotion on a consistent basis, you cannot absorb this knowledge. This is not knowledge for the mind; it is food for the soul. You can only know it through direct experience, not through an intellectual understanding.

In time, when the static of the mind is dampened through entering into the fourth stage of this journey, you will see in all the events and scenes of your life, both large and small, the sure and silent, inexorable workings of the law of synchronicity and hidden coherence woven throughout. If you have not consciously started to master this great journey of life, begin today. Through introspection, yearning, prayer and meditation, your dormant inner power awakens and begins a magnificent journey.

STAGE 1: AWAKEN THE INTUITIVE EXPLOSION

The Eastern tradition

The Eastern tradition speaks of a dormant energy lying asleep within each of us. This energy is as potent as the force that creates and sustains the universe. Humans cannot realize their own potential fully unless this inner power is awakened. Without consciously awakening this energy, human beings mostly exist in a mental state that fluctuates like an emotional yo-yo between fear and joy, loss and gain, success and failure. Nonetheless, due to its negativity, the human mind resists beginning this wondrous journey of awakening.

The power of spirit is known to spiritual seekers of all cultures and religious backgrounds. In the Chinese tradition, it is called chi; to Christians it is known as the Holy Spirit. Hindus call this power, Kundalini, and the Masons speak of the energy as the Spirit Fire (which Mozart, in his opera The Magic Flute, symbolized as a spiritual trial by fire).

In different traditions, there are descriptions of differing methods used to awaken this supreme power. In the Christian tradition, as stated by St Teresa de Avila, devotional prayer and meditation awaken this spiritual energy. If one is without the guidance of a teacher on earth then God's grace, working alone through the power of devotion and meditation, will awaken this dormant energy to serve as your inner guide.

The Eastern philosophers speak of a physical connection of the human mind and consciousness and relate its integration to seven physical locations along the spinal cord. Whether they are understood as actual or mental/metaphysical locations, this analogy is a useful device to visualize the progression of the spirit's individual journey. Chi is defined as the supreme energy that lies dormant at the base of the spine. When she is aroused, she travels upward on a path through the spiritual body parallel with the spine.

Through the guidance of a teacher, the grace of God, and the devotional effort of the individual, this awakened supreme force starts the journey upward.

The Western tradition

St Teresa of Avila's book *The Interior Castle* is a clear and comprehensible Western account of the soul's trek through the seven stages. She refers to the spiritual journey in metaphor as a passing through an interior region of consciousness subdivided into seven mansions or stages of spiritual awakening.

In the first mansion, there are evil tendencies or spirits that attempt to prevent the soul from passing on to the next higher level. These evil tendencies are likened to poisonous creatures; thus, the journeying spirit, at one time or another, is bitten.

In the first mansion, these tendencies will trick you and leave you with a strong desire to be 'righteous and good.' Due to this righteousness and your limited understanding in this primary stage, evil results can be produced.

There are few mansions within the interior castle that are free from struggle with these evil tendencies or mental devils. The devils of the mind are clever, often disguising themselves as angels of light and truth. The seeker must be on guard against the clever, deceitful ways of these entities of the psyche.

The human perspective, your work benefits

Gaining the power of self-knowledge: Through spiritual awakening, the power of learning is magnified, and one may acquire new skills without direct schooling. Your aptitude for self-knowledge is raised. You will find yourself doing things you didn't know you could do, such as writing, painting, or developing a new perspective and a deep insight into your specific profession or field of endeavour.

It is amazing that, when our Rainmaker came to the village, he immediately identified the problem that caused the drought. How could he have known that disharmony was the root cause of the problem since he did not conduct a scientific psychological analysis of the villagers?

Gaining extraordinary insight into your work: Your intuition expands. Whatever you are, whatever you do, you will do it better than before. Take, for example, the Virgin Group which owns Virgin Records, Virgin Airlines, and many other enterprises. This organization is the brainchild of founder Richard Branson. Richard admits that with many of the companies and new ventures he has started, he and his associates did not calculate the sales figures or make projections in advance. They would just feel there was room in the market for their new enterprise!

How is one to teach students in the Harvard Business School's MBA program to 'feel' a business opportunity? They may believe that projected figures on a financial sheet are a valid reference source, when in actuality they are just an educated guess. 'Feeling right,' when it is rooted in intuition and self-knowledge, may be a more valid reference point when it comes to providing direction for a new project.

If, in 1950, the Noble Prize Laureate, Mother Teresa, had asked a business consultant for help in starting her nonprofit charitable work in India, the consultant would have told her to forget it. However, she followed her intuition, and her good work spread to over 137 countries.

Common phenomena

Physical: In the first stage of prayer and meditation, you may find that your head is drowsy and heavy. Your body may begin to swing naturally. Upon the opening of the first spiritual seal one often feels a burning sensation or pain at the base of the spine.

Mental: People who experience the first stage are aware that they can do everything in their life a little better. There is a transformation from their 'normal' self into a much more powerful individual. However, this is not always a blessing for the people around them. At this stage, you feel the intense desire to do good, to do the right thing. You have no tolerance for anything that is not considered a clear-cut, simple 'goodness.'

St Teresa gave a few examples from her own experience. She spoke of her yearnings to do penance and achieve control over her lower nature by torturing herself. In the end, she ruined her health. She also recounted her desire to pursue 'righteous' perfection in others, appointing herself the professional fault-finder in the nunnery. Upon spotting the slightest weakness or fault in others, she would run immediately to report the transgressor to her Prioress. At this stage, one clearly sees the faults of others, but is yet unable to see one's own faults.

Spiritual: Depending on their individual temperament, some people in this state see what they may identify as past events or as events still to happen in the future. A person who does not see these phenomenal manifestations should not consider his or her awareness as inferior. It only means that these phenomena would serve no useful purpose for that individual soul.

The heart is full of devotion. Nevertheless, an individual at this stage of awakening is saturated with pride and ignorance. God is kind to beginners and usually gives them a preview of how good things can get upon the fulfillment of their spiritual success journey.

Beware

For one to seek manifestations as a result of spiritual discovery is to be caught in delusion. Phenomena should not be sought, nor should they be feared if they come unbidden. Then they will not become a stumbling block on your path to spiritual realization.

The combination of a newly acquired awareness of power and a strong desire for goodness, topped with arrogance, pride, delusion, and ignorance, causes many people in this state of awakening to become a nuisance to themselves and others. They view life from a strong, morally righteous position of right and wrong. Most of the time, they believe that they are right and others are wrong. They may feel that they love God and hate everyone else. Ironically, churches and temples are often full of this kind of 'opinionated' people.

However, as anyone who has gone through this stage knows, it is pointless to oppose people in this state or to try to talk any sense into them. Their righteous ignorance will naturally diminish as their unfoldment continues. This stage is not to be considered inferior; it is a road that almost everyone has to travel on his or her journey to the Infinite.

STAGE 2: IGNITE THE CREATIVE FIREWORKS

The Eastern tradition

This supreme energy brings your hidden negative emotions and physical problems to the surface. Since you have previously had a preview of all the wonderful insights that this energy will make available to you further on, this energy is now going to help you get down to business and do some serious surgery. This centre is identified physically with the area in the body of the sacrum. As it is related to your sexual energy, you often experience intense sexual arousal.

At this level, one can become exasperated and downright nasty toward others. While you used to be able to skillfully hide the six deadly human enemies, pride, lust, anger, jealousy, greed and delusion, you find that these qualities are now being magnified in their last gasp for life, sensing that they are soon to be eradicated.

When you are at this pressure point, your friends probably have a hard time putting up with you, and worst of all, you cannot stand yourself. It seems that everything in your life, inside and outside, is going in the wrong direction. You feel great despair. George Washington went through this stage during wartime. His inner enemies and the outer enemy were attacking him from all directions.

The Western tradition

The souls who reach the second level or mansion have a much tougher time than those in the first mansion, who are usually left deaf and dumb by their own ignorance so that they cannot hear the call of the Lord. The souls in the second mansion are now more in tune with the Lord's voice. They hear His call through inspirational words from good friends, spiritual books, or life's hard lessons of sickness and trial.

They then start to recognize their own despicable conduct and thoughts, and fall into confusion and melancholy. They can no longer live in their blissful ignorance and pretentious virtue while condemning the rest of the human race as 'poor sinners.'

When the Divine Spirit lives as a close neighbour, His light is more intense; the reality of good and evil, black and white, is no longer so clearly defined. As these souls make advances toward self-discovery, they become more confused than ever. Stretched between their own positive and negative emotions, they want to do God's bidding, but they are betrayed by their senses.

The human perspective, your work benefits

Redesigning your life, a time of trial and tribulation:
This is a serious reorganization period in your life. You may
lose your job and have health problems, family problems, or
problems with your relationships. Through the grace of your
own desire to improve, God has answered you. You are on a
correction course and beginning to design and redesign your
life. This is a time of trial and tribulation, a time of career
change and much instability. It looks as if your life is falling
apart. In fact, it is only in the process of being redirected and
reorganized for the better. The unproductive old way has to be
torched to make room for the new. In time, all will be well.

Outrageously creative ideas burst forth from nowhere:
As the second stage is rooted in the sexual power and human
sexual drive, it is the foundation of all creativity. Out of sexual
urge, human and artistic life is created.

When your life is presented with great challenges, it also
provides you with great tools for overcoming the adversities.
At this stage, you have no idea from where your fantastically
brilliant ideas have come. Your dynamo of creativity is rushing
forward with a furious force.

Common phenomena

Physical: Whatever latent physical weakness you have, will
be surfacing so that it can be expelled permanently. Now, this
next statement may become a cause for controversy, however,
I am stating it here as a guidepost for those who have these
experiences and feel they have somehow deviated from
the path.

As stage two is associated with the sacrum area, you may find yourself sexually charged up during this period. Sometimes when you meditate, you may become sexually aroused, finding your mind filled with sensual thoughts, instead of experiencing sweet bliss.

Do not think you have fallen from grace. This is a natural phenomenon associated with this level and needs to be understood in the context of your overall journey. Hold steady to your course and all will be understood in time. God's nature is joy and this is a valid association and expression.

Mental: In the past, through your desire to do the right thing and to be good, you often sacrificed your own interests. Now, due to past self-suppression, your irritation, anger and resentment have surfaced uncontrollably. These abhorrent, atavistic, petty-minded emotions scream for your attention and refuse to be pushed aside or forced under the surface any longer. You feel guilty and shameful about your 'ignoble' emotions running rampant.

With continuous self-effort, you move forward into this stage. Or rather, it is not so much you who has moved forward; to be more accurate, you get moved. God is touched by your willingness to know Him, so He gives you a kick from behind; and before you know it, your comfortable life has turned into chaos and uncertainty.

Spiritual: The second mansion leaves one in a very vulnerable spiritual state, knowing too much to return to a life of the 'norm,' but also aware that one has a long, hard journey before being able to bask in the divine sunlight.

Through introspection you will see occasional glimpses of the bliss of the upcoming fourth stage to signal to you that you are on the right track, so this period is not cloaked all in dark. Cling tight to God; His grace will propel you forward.

Beware

In general, this is a very depressing stage. This is a period of inner cleansing. Hidden mental and physical diseases are surfacing in order to be discarded. The good aspect is that your Maker will surely be with you and carry you on His broad shoulders to help you through it.

Any negative experiences that result from the unfolding of the seven spiritual stages, will all diminish eventually as your hidden, defective character impressions surface and expel themselves outwards. There is nothing you have to do to try to correct your negativities. As long your heart is on a positive journey and vigilantly striving to improve your every action and thought, in time, your negativities will all disappear on their own accord. On the other hand, all of your positive experiences will intensify as you continually travel upwards.

However, if you practice mediation intensely, you can shorten your times of trial. Beware, you cannot meditate ten hours a day in hopes of accelerating the process. It does not work that way. Just as a small voltage box cannot withstand a high volume of electricity, in the same way, the unprepared human cannot hold an excessive amount of spiritual energy by artificially imposing long hours of meditative discipline. Humans need to gradually expand their spiritual container to be able to hold the overwhelming divine energy.

STAGE 3: EXPLORE THE POWERHOUSE OF FEARLESSNESS

The Eastern tradition

When you have entered the third stage, it does not mean that you have passed irretrievably beyond the first and second stages. This stage is physically associated with the navel, the power centre. At times, you will still be subject to the tests of temptation from the mental patterns and behaviour of the first two stages. As you police yourself and practice self-correction, in time it will become harder and harder for the ego-devils to push you backwards. Then you will start to witness the initial battles.

What I mean by a battle between the stages is that, while you are working in the third stage, frequently you will move into the fourth stage and experience a bubbling up of spontaneous love for no apparent reason. You might be in the middle of an argument and suddenly feel, at the same time, great love for the very person that you're arguing with.

The Western tradition

The soul has struggled through the first two mansions, and that was no small task. There is much of grace to uplift you during your dangerous passage on this spiritual journey. As the soul drinks of the divine nectar, it gains the lustre of wisdom and begins to scintillate with joy.

At this stage the soul is restless, though it strives to gain humility and gratitude, and prays for the power of complete surrender to God and the acceptance of God's tests and guidance. The Lord wishes to take complete possession of the soul to help it reach perfection. The human being sincerely wishes to follow God's will, and the battle for surrender begins. It is not because the human soul does not want to surrender to God's guidance; rather, the temptations of the flesh are still imposing their influence.

The human perspective, your work benefits

Fearlessness and resilience: These are trying times, the necessary processing period for the dross iron of your human soul to be transformed into the steel blade of spirit. During this period, you reveal to yourself what you are made of. During these times of trial, life will bash you around, pull you apart, and put you back together, again and again. Through this, life will teach you humility, flexibility, fearlessness, and resilience. These qualities will benefit your future greatly. As Wal-Mart's CEO, David Glass, said about Sam Walton, the founder, "Sam's greatest strength was fearlessness. He'd foul up something embarrassingly, then come in the next day raring to go with something else." Our beloved George Washington also continuously fouled up battles, yet he charged on. George went through the trials of this phase and gained the power of fearlessness.

Willingness to take on new, untried tasks: Through your inner journey of confronting fear, you are no longer fearful. After considering risks, you are now more willing to explore untried ventures. By doing so, your electrifying destiny will be unveiled to you.

Common phenomena

Physical: The body is still going through the second stage of purification, and at this stage the digestive fire becomes purified and strengthened.

Mental: You are tired of feeling anger, resentment, and guilt. You are even more tired of putting yourself down and making yourself wrong for feeling those emotions. You have pulled opened the dark curtain of your subconscious and have found it full of cobwebs, dust, and dirt. Now you are struggling to accept yourself for who you are. It is too late to return to your blissfully ignorant ways of pretentious, self-righteous 'goodness and sweetness.'

The way to expedite your progress into the fourth stage is through the practice of surrender, of letting the human ego go out of the way and making way for God's light, knowing that whatever happens occurs for a valid, mysterious reason.

To put this concept into terse language, when most people enter upon the spiritual journey, in the first stage their life 'works.' When they progress to the second stage, their life falls apart. Courageously moving on to the third stage, they begin to rebuild their lives and to shape their reality in a more suitable direction, whether this manifests through career, health, or personal relationships.

Spiritual: Because this centre deals with power and fearlessness, often your deepest fears are confronted. One of my friends would see ghosts whenever he sat down to meditate. He became so disturbed with this manifestation that he quit and never meditated again. Whatever image frightens you most may appear to challenge you.

Once, during my own mediation, I saw a female ghost with long, loose black hair and a green face with blood dripping out of her mouth and her tongue hanging out. I was too scared and powerless to move. I screamed and screamed until my husband ran in and turned on the light. Abruptly, the spectre disappeared. Later I realized that the image I had seen was not a ghost but the image of the Eastern tradition's Divine Mother in Her form as the Destroyer of the World.

In fact, seeing demon-like apparitions and elements of the spirit world is a common experience. The result is that this makes you fearless, strong and whole. Even Christ had to fight off the demons and the devil after he had fasted for forty days in the desert before starting his ministry.

The soul is working on some of the heavy-duty human character defects, such as hatred, fear and treachery. Also, at this stage, your willpower is being purified. You become more obstinate and much more focused on the application of your will.

Beware

The movement from stages one through four normally does not happen as a clearly defined, smooth passage from one stage to the next. The energy may be focused on one major centre while, simultaneously, the energy is working on higher and lower centres to a lesser degree.

Many people have set forth rumours that when you meditate, your experience will be very peaceful. These rumours have caused great anxiety for people who, committed to meditation and the path of spirituality, find themselves more restless and irritated than ever. In fact, this is why it is sometimes said that the path of spirituality is as painful as walking upon a razor's edge.

This is not due, as some think, to the erroneous idea that the more you meditate, the more restless you become. It is like a top that, when spinning at high speed, looks as though it were motionless. When the top starts to slow down, you see it to begin to wobble and make wild, erratic, swinging motions.

The mind is much the same. When you first begin meditation, your mind is racing so fast that you cannot sense its restlessness. Through years of practicing meditation, the mind comes more under control and, like a slowing top, wobbles and quivers.

However, in despair, many people give up meditation at this point, feeling that it is better to live in ignorance of the spirit than to continue a life of making themselves and others around them miserable. Now is the time one needs to muster the courage to go forth. Know that the presence of these symptoms indicates that you are doing well. Before the sun rises, the darkest hour is just before dawn.

STAGE 4: FIND THE TREASURE CHEST OF LOVE

The Eastern tradition

The fourth spiritual centre, the gateway between our lower and higher natures, is located at the heart level. Unlike the centres that have come before, which mostly deal with conquering negative qualities, this centre is mixed with both good and not-so-good qualities.

The good qualities include hope, caring, and discrimination. Your senses start to come under control; your actions begin to stem from noble and pure motives. In the heart, one can hear the divine inner sounds, called *nada* in Sanskrit. These divine sounds enchant the mind and captivate the heart to make the concentration of the practitioner one-pointed and accelerate the experience of the great joy of the soul.

You are now less judgmental about yourself and others. The wisdom of love has entered your heart. Your old 'ill-fitting' friends will drop out of your life. They will reject you and make sure you know that it was your fault they are leaving you.

You have outgrown them. Now it is time for you to move on. If they had been capable of seeing and acknowledging that, they would not be your old 'ill-fitting' friends. They would have progressed spiritually beside you.

Mysterious is the way of self-unfolding. The fourth stage is the gateway to universal love. When one is completely rooted in stage four, the heart opens and the light of love comes pouring through. You feel great empathy and compassion for the human condition. Ironically, until you are solidly established in the third stage, love cannot surface fully. Love is this delicate human emotion that needs to be protected by your strength. Everyone speaks of love as the most powerful force on earth. This is so because love is rooted in the soil of power. You need to be grounded in power. Only then are you powerful enough to unconditionally open to experience love.

The Western tradition

Normally, entering into this mansion requires the dedication of many years of intense spiritual practice. However, there are always those persons who are the exception, for everything is possible in the misty, uncharted realms of God.

In this fourth mansion, you will experience a sublime sweetness during your prayer and meditation. Often your heart will fill with a tender joy that will make you sob for no reason. These are not the tears of sadness but of celebration. These experiences should be greatly prized, for they are gifts from the divine. When people access the heart centre, they shed tears of great joy.

At this stage, St Teresa speaks of the inner music that all meditators and saints from all of the world's religious disciplines have experienced. She says: "As I write this, the noise in my head is so loud that I am beginning to wonder what is going on in it. My head sounds as if it were full of brimming rivers, and then, as if all the water in those rivers came suddenly rushing downward; and a host of little birds seem to be whistling, not in the ears, but in the upper part of the head, where the higher part of the soul is said to be. I have heard, indeed, that some persons find [through spiritual practices] they produce a constriction of the chest and even involuntary bodily movements that are so violent as to cause the blood to gush from the nose and produce other, similarly disconcerting symptoms."

The human perspective, your work benefits

Desire to truly serve your fellow beings: People are in business for profit, but profit for profit's sake alone gives no satisfaction to the human soul. When your heart is opened, you begin to hold a universal viewpoint of how your work can affect the world positively and negatively.

A salesman sells his products by being motivated to provide a solution for his potential customers. A business owner, while making a profit, is also interested in the well-being of his staff, his community, and the world in which he lives. The more people there are who operate their lives and their businesses from this level of spiritual understanding, the better our world will be.

Mr Chen Wun-yu is the founder of the Taiwan Know-You Seed Company. He is an internationally renowned vegetable breeder, the father of the seedless watermelon, and a major supplier of first-class vegetable seeds worldwide. In the early 1980s, he decided to open a joint venture company with the government of Thailand to grow vegetable seeds in the northern part of the country.

Although the printed business plan regarding this joint venture sounded totally 'businesslike,' Mr Chen told me privately that the real motivation for opening up the new operation was to bring economic growth as a means of securing peace and stability in northern Thailand, which is vulnerable to Cambodian, Laotian, and Chinese Communist penetration. Mr Chen allocated a certain dollar amount for the operation. If the operation failed, he told me, so be it. He would have done what he thought was the right thing. The operation was intended to save others, but it turned out to be a self-preservation device.

From the mid-1960s through to the mid-1980s, Taiwan had a steady, abundant harvest of vegetable seeds. However, from the mid-1980s to the present, Taiwan has consistently had more years of crop failures than harvests, thanks to typhoons. Mr Chen told me it was a good thing that he had the seed harvest from Thailand; otherwise, he would have had to close his doors long ago.

The quality of your service will soar: No matter what industry you are working in, good customer service is essential to the financial well-being of your business. Millions of dollars are spent each year in corporate training in the attempt to improve the quality of customer service.

These training courses only teach the workers how to act, not how to increase their affinity for their customers. Love and respect are the essential ingredients of good customer service. Without genuine love, you are merely going through the motions. Guided by empathy, how can you possibly be wrong in the service of your customers?

Your intuition will be sharpened: At this stage, you have gone through trial-and-error and corrected your work. You have learned how to listen to the voice of your intuition and to recognize when your mind is providing you with foolish ideas.

Your intuition is identified as that clear, inner voice that does not cloud your mind or enhance your confusion. It is that single voice that vibrates steadily in your heart. It provides comfort and assurance instead of chaos. With it, you can experience future events as if they had happened yesterday. You gain confidence in your ability to depend on your intuitive guidance as a legitimate decision-making source for your business.

Common phenomena

Physical, spontaneous yoga movement: Whether you are a Christian mystic, a Eastern yogi, or a Buddhist mediator, you will undergo a similar experience. All hear the inner music, as St Teresa described it, and go through the purification of the body, mind and soul by having involuntary body movements, called kriyas.

In fact, these involuntary body movements were the origin of the physical branch of the science of yoga called Hatha Yoga. In ancient times, when the spiritual seekers meditated for extensive periods, they found that their bodies would twist involuntarily into different shapes.

These involuntary movements are guided by the inner, all-knowing divine force that is totally aware of which part of a seeker's body needs to be purified. That force will place the body in the necessary position without human intervention or effort.

Later, when human beings wanted to purify and strengthen their bodies, they began to mimic these divinely inspired movements and to train their bodies into these twisting and strengthening positions.

Physical, the synchronization of the menopausal: We are all spiritual beings, even if we have never meditated, prayed, or made any spiritual effort at all, just as a lion cub will always be a lion cub, even if it is raised by sheep and erroneously thinks it is a lamb. Our genetic imprint has programmed us unfailingly to seek our connection with our Maker in spite of ourselves.

With the increasing number of baby-boomers entering the age of menopause, more interest is being focused on this topic. Many books and articles speak of the silent suffering that women have to endure due to their biochemical changes.

At one time, I could not understand why God imposed so much seemingly unnecessary pain upon females. No wonder some deluded Buddhists are convinced that only an inferior soul takes birth in a female form. (I will dispose of that ludicrous theory in my next book, *The Working Woman's Art of War*.) For the time being, my focus is: What is the purpose of menopause? During my meditations, the answer came to me.

As females have a genetic propensity to be tender, caring, and intuitive, they are more suited to ensure the perpetuation of the human race. God has allocated thirty to forty years of a woman's life to fulfilling her reproductive opportunity. Once this period is over, the female no longer has to deal with the 'nuisance' of reproductive obligation. Her genetic programming is then refocused onto the more vital issue of discovering herself and her Maker.

During a female's reproductive period, her energy resources are centred on the lower part of her body to ensure the fulfillment of her genetic potential. In other words, her energy is focused on the lower three centres, the survival centres, to ensure the best possible opportunity for the survival of her infant and herself. When the window of time for reproduction is closed, the natural energy shoots up to the heart and forces it open to become sweeter and softer inside.

During the menopausal period, a woman often feels tearful, and her chest feels tight, full of restless energies. These are the same symptoms that St Teresa of Avila described for the progression of the spiritual seeker. Because the heart is the storage house of suppressed emotions, when the concentrated energy enters the heart to do its housecleaning, the settled dust starts flying and great mood swings occur.

By fulfilling the reproductive function, the female is detoured from her original purpose in life, to experience her own divinity. So Mother Nature gives women a jump start after they enter menopause to help them clear the lower three centres and work out the impurities in the heart centre. Often this process can be overwhelming for those who have not devoted any time to the spiritual pursuit. The source of their tears is misidentified as negative emotion.

For those who have been earnestly cultivating energy in self-cleansing, menopausal symptoms are familiar friends, and tearfulness comes mostly from being overwhelmed by the emotion of love. This does not lessen their power to conduct their worldly affairs. On the contrary, it greatly empowers them. As the lower parts of energy move upward into the heart and higher regions, the conflicts of their inner struggle are lessened.

The symptoms, such as tearfulness and tightness of the chest, are also present in males when they enter the fourth stage and their heart has been cracked open. However, men often try to suppress these emotions when they feel overwhelming joy bubbling up in their hearts.

Mental: As an eminent master once said, "For contentment to arise within, you must love your own soul intensely." Stage four involves the recognition and acceptance of your imperfect perfection. You are able to accept yourself (and others) because the joy of spiritual contentment is the wellspring of your love.

As your heart opens and is filled with love, you rediscover your own power. Now you will become sweeter, but more powerful than ever. Without knowing one's own power, one is incapable of giving love. As a child of our Creator, each individual has the complete power and capacity to give and receive love without hesitation.

Spiritual: The opening of the heart centre will give you the power to spiritually travel throughout the universe. However, this is only a minor sideshow. Most importantly, love will begin to pour into your life. This is the goal of meditation, not to see mystical phenomena or obtain supernatural powers, but to know love.

Beware

Even though you have entered the fourth stage, the demands of the lower stages are not completely eradicated. You still have to be vigilant to guard against the negative intruders.

In general, all is going very well for you. While religious leaders fight over who owns God, spiritual seekers from every path have found that God leads them to Him through different maps that chart the same territory.

STAGE 5: INCREASE COMMUNICATION SKILLS NATURALLY

The Eastern tradition

This centre is located at the level of the throat. Here your mind begins to experience peace. When this centre is totally purified, you become a benevolent person and an excellent communicator.

Words flow effortlessly out of your mouth or onto paper. Your taste becomes refined; even the simplest of foods tastes delicious. At this centre, seekers begin to smell the divine fragrance from within. They acquire the true vision of the universe, seeing everything in the world as a scintillating light that reflects God's glory. Once a great teacher was asked why he wore dark glasses all the time. He answered, "Because everyone is so radiant."

The Western tradition

All of one's prayers have led to this point, and the individual is about to undergo a transformation. St Teresa explained this stage as the human soul about to shed the old, just as a silkworm comes out of its cocoon as a little white butterfly. The silkworm must die before the butterfly can come out. With us, the death comes more easily when we can see ourselves living a new life. The duty at this stage is to be willing to die to your old life of your own free will.

I am not speaking here of physical death but of the death of the small human ego to which we all so tightly cling. This ego is our familiar friend and the reference point from which we have addressed all of our human encounters from the time of birth. This ego separates us as individual survival centres. Skillfully optimizing for individual survival, it has isolated us from universal brotherhood. It is hard to let an old friend die. This is the bottleneck in the transformation of a human being into a Divine being.

The human perspective, your work benefits

Increasing your verbal communication skills naturally: Perfecting communication skills will make you an effective salesman. Eighty percent of business is about one human being attempting to communicate with another. Whatever your service or product, communication is the key that turns the engine. When you speak, your words will flow effortlessly. The aim of your communication will naturally include a consideration of the other's well-being.

Unleash your writing ability: Without you going to school to learn the craft of writing, words and ideas will flow naturally and prolifically from your pen.

Expand your skill of naturally knowing: You will acquire complex knowledge without learning it from books or school. You will have a direct perception of worldly knowledge in your chosen field or a field in which you had never thought you would be interested. In reality, everything you ever needed to know has always been within you. Just think about this: who was the teacher who taught the first teacher on the earth? That teacher learned from no one but herself or himself.

In the Vatican, on the ceiling of the Sistine Chapel, there is a painting by Michelangelo of a non-Christian female figure, Delphica, a Greek high priestess and prophetess who was the

Oracle at Delphi. The scene shows her reading from the scriptures just as something suddenly distracts her. She turns to look aside while her hands are still holding the book.

For centuries, experts have agreed on the significance and meaning of this painting: Michelangelo was telling the world that although the information in the book of knowledge is important, when God Himself comes to give the oracle a direct experience of His wisdom, she turns away from the book and chooses to follow the divine direct experience.

Our Rainmaker also attained this state. For him to know what caused the drought was extremely insightful and profound. This is not an ordinary knowledge. Ancient scriptures also state that the cause of natural disaster is due to the collective consciousness being out of harmony with God, nature and man. So humans create their own natural disasters. However, our Rainmaker didn't learn this from scripture. His source was the knowledge within himself. If he had merely read about it, he would not have completely possessed the knowledge and know how to correct the course of events.

Common phenomena

Physical: You will encounter other phenomena than only the sharpening of one's taste buds, the emanation of the divine fragrance, and superb communication skills.

As the old and the unworthy fall by the wayside, you will draw new and exciting people and events into your life, for like attracts like. You will develop your natural power of self-assurance. Your thoughts will become steady. Your actions will be in harmony with your inner guidance.

Mental: At this stage, people see their fellow beings with the eyes of equality. It is not an easy state of attainment. The concept of all people being created equal is a noble idea, but we mortals often fall far short of that. We are the animal that constantly judges how others fit in and how we fit within the whole scope of social and business structures.

Spiritual: At the fifth stage, you gain the profound power to tear the veil of the dualistic power of maya, the delusive power that causes us to see inequality in the world. You judge how successful you are by comparing yourself (and your bank account) to those whom you consider successful. Then you know whether you should feel superior or inferior at any given time. By conquering the power of maya, you never again have the feelings of being inferior or superior. You realize that as a divine creation of our Maker, you and everyone else are always superior.

Maya is a Sanskrit word meaning the power that creates human delusion. Instead of seeing the world with equal vision, we experience it from a judgmental, dualistic viewpoint. The following story illustrates the meaning of *maya*.

Once there was a very prestigious club that one could not enter unless one were a lord or lady. However, this presented a problem. If everyone inside was a lord or lady who expected to be served and waited on, where would the cook come from, or the waiters, or the janitors?

Being wise lords and ladies, they hit upon the solution that they would take turns in performing the service jobs. This week, one would be the janitor while another would be the cook. The following week, the one who had played the role of janitor would relax and be waited on. The week after, he or she would be the waiter. Thus, all the lords and ladies enjoyed themselves as they took their turns in each position, high and low.

This is the way the world looks to people who possess equal vision beyond the influence of *maya*. All men and women are equal as children of our Creator, and we are simply given our respective roles to play. It is not the relative importance of the role in the earthly drama that matters, but the skill and enthusiasm with which one expresses the divine spiritual qualities in the faithful performance of those God-assigned duties.

Beware

At this stage you may experience neck or throat discomfort. It is all part of the cleansing process. At any stage of this journey, whenever you find yourself feeling physical discomfort, do see a physician first. Often a physical sickness has a spiritual connection as spiritual infirmity can manifest through physical forms.

STAGE 6: ENJOY THE PEACE OF EQUAL VISION

The Eastern tradition

Ajna means 'command,' and this level is so named because no one can move beyond this point unless he has received the grace or command of God. This centre is located between the eyebrows.

This centre controls the mind. When you focus your attention on this point, you fall easily into meditation. When this centre opens up, the delusion is broken that you are separate from your Maker and the rest of the world. You start to experience living in the state of unity. At this point, the mind becomes contented, for the soul begins to experience divine unity with the whole universe.

The Western tradition

The soul has arrived at the next-to-final mansion. The spirit is yearning for divine union with her beloved. At this stage, the soul recognizes the call of the Lord, and the spirit takes leave of the body for moments at a time to be united with her Lord.

St Teresa described the rapture of her out-of-body experience in this way: "For when He means to enrapture this soul, it loses its power of breathing, with the result that, although its other senses sometimes remain active a little longer, it cannot possibly speak. At other times it loses all its power at once, and the hands and the body grow so cold that the body seems no longer to have a soul, sometimes it even seems doubtful if there is any breath in the body." Even when one returns to the consciousness of the body, one is still absorbed for a long time in ecstasy.

This stage has been experienced by many practitioners. The out-of-body experience is more common than many people realize. It does not happen because the persons who experience it are near enlightenment; this experience is available to all who seek it with devotion and the guidance of God because our Maker likes to give previews in order to encourage us to stay on this spiritual journey. St Teresa was firmly grounded in this stage. She was a permanent resident, while many others who have experienced this out-of-body experience are occasional visitors to this sixth mansion.

All scriptures of every spiritual discipline say the same thing: you will not know it is true until you have experienced it. I speak of this from the experiences that I have had. While great beings are constantly living in this ecstatic state, I and countless others have been given glimpses a few times, and from those experiences I can assure you that this is a place that is well worth your utmost human effort to strive to reach.

Human perspective, benefit to your work

There is nothing left to do: The world of 'yours' and 'mine' has dissolved. At this point, 'your' work and 'your' world have disappeared. Everything you do is done for the good of all, to maintain the cosmic order. The world receives untold benefits just from the existence of such a person whose heart is truly pure, good, and steady. In India, Mother Teresa was an example of one for whom, out of her focus on God alone, all things were done naturally.

God becomes your business partner: I have told many people privately, and this is a good place to state it publicly, "A good book is greater than its author." Any good book is the result of a partnership between the author and God's inspiration; the author set his or her ego aside and opens a route to receive the message from higher up. The same concept holds for the creation of any great artistic, scientific, or business venture.

Common phenomena

Physical: There are physical discomforts that come with this stage. To different degrees, people will feel a buzzing sensation or a piercing pain between the eyebrows, inside the eyeballs, or along the temples. Sometimes a buzzing sensation or heat is felt at the top of the forehead, but a doctor can find nothing wrong with the eyes.

Mental: At this stage, you find a new surge of inner harmony, the unfamiliar emotions of peace and tranquillity. You begin to experience genuine spiritual compassion for others. You recognize that the flame of love that is burning within you is equally present in others, even though they may not have perceived it in themselves.

Spiritual: At this stage, the power of omniscience begins to arise which allows you to know other people's thoughts. Whenever a spirit has evolved to a high state of realization, heaven and earth rejoice and mankind benefits from this individual's existence. The Renaissance painters expressed this idea so beautifully in their portrayal of the saints, showing the angels singing in great joy while the clouds open and joy pours forth.

Beware

During meditation, when you focus your attention on a fixed position between your eyes, you may have a terrific headache. If this happens, let your attention focus on your heart, navel, or just above your sexual organ, wherever it feels best. Eventually, when you are firmly established in this stage, you will be pulled involuntarily to rest your gaze between the eyebrows. It will then be comfortable. Everything will happen in good time.

STAGE 7: BECOME ONE WITH THE CREATOR

The Eastern tradition

The Great Hindu, Saint Jnaneshwari, spoke of this state: "After a seeker is fully established in this centre, he reaches out with the arms of awareness of the united individual soul and the supreme Creator." Just as water from the ocean evaporates into clouds and then pours down into the ocean as rain, in the same way the individual soul, having lived in the body, now reenters a partnership with the supreme Maker.

A great meditation teacher recounts his experience in this way: "There are a thousand knots in the sahasrara [located at the top of the head], which shine with the brilliance of a thousand suns, but instead of being scorching like the sun, their light is cooling. When I saw that brilliance within myself, I fell down, because I could not bear its intensity. In the centre of that effulgence lies a fascinatingly beautiful light. Sometimes it comes out of the eyes and stands in front of you. It moves with the speed of lightning, and it is subtle such that when it passes through the eye, the eye doesn't feel its movement. Everyone should see this [light] at least once."

This shimmering light is the form of God that lives within us. In this light is contained the whole of the universe. This is what Christ referred to when He stated that "the kingdom of heaven is within you." If you have never experienced the kingdom of heaven within, how can you think you will know heaven just because you have dropped your 'old clothing,' your old and diseased body? You have to see it at least once in your life. As I said many times before, our Maker is so generous, before we are worthy of this profound experience, He will give us the preview of all the good things to come.

At this magnificent stage, the soul does not experience a separation from God. As there is no separation, there is no difference between the states of rapture and normality. In the previous stages, one has had to go into a state of trance or have an out-of-body experience to be with God. Now one is with God all the time, even while performing daily, mundane duties. According to the East, this state is called sahaj samadhi, the walking ecstasy, because we are at one with God's intense joy, whether eating, sleeping, working, or talking.

The Western tradition

The small white butterfly now has died and merged into His Majesty, the Dweller in the Seventh Mansion. The person who is in this state finds himself better in every way. As St Paul said, "He who is joined to God becomes one Spirit with Him." St Paul was referring to this experience of union between the individual soul and its Creator.

Unlike the other mansions, in which the soul is always in conflict and experiencing trials and weariness, now all of the human sense faculties and passions are in a state of profound peace. This does not mean that the normal condition of human existence, with all its trials and afflictions, has ceased in your life. It means that the chaos and trials of life have no power over you in the least, and their transitory tempests do not alter your blissful inner peace.

At this stage, the soul is totally detached from the world. It wishes to be in solitude or performs actions only to help others to reach their highest unfolding. At this point, the soul welcomes whatever experiences in life God brings to it. As the Noble Peace Prize winner, Mother Teresa, said, even her ill health was God's gift to her. This complete spiritual journey took St Teresa of Avila approximately forty years of her life.

The human perspective, the benefit to your work

When you are a Christ-like being, who needs ten thousand soldiers or workers? When you become that power, every force within the universe is ready to serve you at your command. The stars are your diamonds, and the sun is your shining ruby.

Great beings from the past and the present have achieved this stage. They have consequently dedicated themselves to the removal of the suffering that most of humanity experiences due to ignorance of the divine association. For their work, their names have been immortalized throughout the ages.

Common phenomena

Physical: The light is God's form dwelling within you. A great teacher said, "You have to see it at least once in your life." It is not a rare phenomenon to see this effulgent light shine out from your eyes and playfully dance in front of you. I have seen it even in the very early stages of my spiritual pursuit.

The shimmering ray has often jumped out and stood in front of my eyes in midair or appeared on the paper while I was reading, or on my computer screen, and then quickly disappeared. This is the hidden meaning of what St Paul stated as: "...it shall be revealed by fire."

God is good to those who seek Him. He knows it is a difficult path. Thus, He will give us signs of encouragement all along the way as gifts to lift us and entice us to stay on the path and to let us know that we are doing well.

The reason the spiritual light often disappears in a flash is that the mind is fickle and unsteady and cannot hold on to such a rare vision. However, when one is firmly established in the seventh level, it will stand still and unveil to the seeker the mysteries of all the worlds.

Mental and Spiritual: At this stage, the mind has dissolved into the Spirit, and there is no longer a division into mental and spiritual realms. Nothing you possess possesses you. You become the master of your universe. You are in the world, but you have also transcended it. The world exists for the sole purpose of pleasing you, and you exist solely to please God and maintain the divine cosmic order. You become the embodiment of that highest code of living, detachment. Prior to this stage, there is attachment in you to varying degrees despite your personal efforts.

CONCLUSION

These seven stages are the complete account of the journey to the supreme, divine success of inner unfoldment. At any given time, you know a portion of yourself, while another portion remains a mystery to you. The degree of ignorance varies with each individual. No stage is to be condemned; they must all be traversed.

Meditation is enjoyable to children because they are naturally close to God. For adults, meditation is a necessary tool because it increases your proliferation in work and decreases your stress, giving you a competitive edge by accessing your inner resources. By contacting God each morning and aligning your physical, mental, and spiritual energy with meditation, you are prepared to face the day and not be swept away by the chaotic details of life. You will not waste all of your energy in just maintaining your sanity.

Meditation in later life is imperative as death is impatiently waiting to snatch you. It is time to prepare for the journey home to meet our Maker. As St Teresa of Avila said, "It is absurd to think that we can enter Heaven without first entering our own souls."

If your objective is not to enter Heaven, but just to do well in life, you will energize your business skill in an extraordinary way, simply by being in touch with the power of the Great Sprit. Our Rainmaker could not have made rain when all other reputable rainmakers had failed at the task, unless he had possessed that power of the Great Spirit.

SUMMARY

These seven stages of spiritual unfolding directly affect one's ability to manifest physical success. As the soul journeys through the seven centres, specific innate talents for mastering attainment in the material world are also unfolding.

Stage 1: Awaken the intuitive explosion

Gaining the power of self-knowledge: The power of learning is magnified, and one may acquire new skills without schooling. The ability of self-knowledge is raised.

Gaining an extraordinary insight toward your work: Whatever you are, whatever you do, you can do it better now than before.

Stage 2: Ignite the creative fireworks

Redesigning your life, a time of trial and tribulation: It looks as if your life is falling apart, but it is only in the process of being redirected and reorganized for the better.

Outrageously creative ideas burst forth from nowhere: When your life is presented with great challenges, it also provides you with great tools for overcoming the adversities.

Stage 3: Explore the powerhouse of fearlessness

Fearlessness and resilience: The dross iron of your human soul is transformed into the steel blade of Spirit. Through this, life will teach you humility, flexibility, fearlessness, and resilience.

Willingness to take on new, untried tasks: After considering risks, you are now more willing to explore untried ventures. By doing so, your electrifying destiny will be unveiled to you.

Stage 4: Find the treasure chest of love

Desire to truly serve your fellow beings: When your heart is opened, you begin to hold a universal viewpoint of how your work can affect the world positively and negatively.

The quality of your service will soar: Love and respect are the essential ingredients of good customer service.

Your intuition will be sharpened: You have learned how to listen to the voice of your intuition and to recognize when your mind is providing you with foolish ideas.

Stage 5: Increase communication skills naturally

Increasing your verbal communication skills naturally: This will make you an effective salesman and perceptive communicator. When you speak, your words will flow effortlessly. The aim of your communication will naturally include a consideration of the other's well-being.

Unleash your writing ability: Without you going to school to learn the craft of writing, words and ideas will flow naturally and prolifically from your pen.

Expand your skill of naturally knowing: You will have a direct perception of worldly knowledge in your chosen field or a field in which you had never thought you would be interested.

Stage 6: Enjoy the peace of equal vision

There is nothing left to do: At this point, 'your' work and 'your' world have disappeared. Everything you do is done for the good of all, to maintain the cosmic order.

God becomes your business partner: A good book is greater than its author. Any good book is the result of a partnership between the author and God's inspiration; the author opens the route to receive a message from higher up. The same thing goes for the creation of any great artistic, scientific, or business venture.

Stage 7: Become one with the Creator

When you are a Christ-like being, who needs ten thousand soldiers or workers? When you become that power, every force within the universe is ready to serve you at your command.

Great beings from the past and the present have achieved this stage. They have consequently dedicated themselves to the removal of the suffering that most of humanity experiences due to ignorance of the divine association. For their work, their names have been immortalized throughout the ages.

Epilogue—let go

Studying and adopting the four secrets of the Rainmaker will lead us to tap into the power of the *law of synchronicity and hidden coherence*. Synchronicity, by my definition as I use it in this work, is the coming together of auspicious persons, events, and elements at just the right time to provide for our successful and desired outcome. When we have prepared ourselves by proper alignment with the universal forces of good, synchronicity happens simply because it happens. Hidden coherence is what most of us call 'good luck' because it is an extraneous event that occurs without being caused or effected by any obvious, outward reason.

By incorporating the four secrets, you will enhance your ability to make the things and events in your life happen perfectly in perfect timing. Since there is no specific formula to precipitate synchronicity and hidden coherence for our benefit, we have only to create the correct environment that attracts miracles to their field of perfect timing. You cannot force or orchestrate this; you can only practice the laws that generate the magnetism which draws these favourable forces.

By practicing and embodying the four secrets of the Rainmaker, you will enhance your opportunity to have the *law of synchronicity and the power of hidden coherence* become a standard occurrence in your life.

Through our human evolution, most of us have formed a belief system that states: "In order to be successful in my work, my life must be painful and filled with struggle." We subconsciously feel that if we do not experience the pain of effort along the way, we will not achieve our goals.

LET GO BY LETTING GO

A couple of days ago, I received a letter from a friend who told me of the struggle in his life. He wrote, "I know my fear of letting go of my effort and struggle is what keeps the struggle and effort in place. Somehow, in my mind, I think letting go of effort and struggle would make my investment of years of tears and my entire existence seem like a waste. My mind feels that if I can be successful without the effort and struggle, it would mean that someone or something else has been in control of my life all along. My ego hates that. I also feel a layer of new fear surfacing, in that if I give up my effort and struggle, God will punish me for not efforting and trying harder."

Our mind is like a computer disk full of ingrained traces. These traces are called *samskaras* in Sanskrit—karmic impressions. In the West, we refer to them as negative programming. For those who believe in reincarnation, the *samskaras* include the billions of impressions gathered from lifetimes before. For those who do not believe that they have ever lived before, the *samskaras* would be the impressions accumulated in this lifetime or inherited through genetic memory.

The more we dwell on the same themes, the more we reinforce our behaviour. The way to let go is to let go. To know the truth of a given situation is to no longer have the need to be run by the falsehood that is its opposite. Freedom is born out of experiencing that there is no need for the suffering and struggle. It is knowing, "I am releasing and letting go."

MAKE GOD YOUR CHAMPION

The Rainmaker's secrets elevate the reader from ordinary material consciousness into an extraordinary state where insights unfold with ease, where we see how the mystical and spiritual elements affect our practical day-to-day world of making a living.

All my life, I have been a fierce fighter. I have always had to claw my way through to gain anything I wanted. Once, during my meditation, a vision came to me. God appeared as the Good Shepherd, and I as His sheep. Sheep do not have to struggle if they are willing to surrender unto the care of the Good Shepherd.

In another vision, I experienced God as my Knight-Protector. He told me that, as the Ultimate Warrior, He should fight my battles, for He is much better at this than I. When I came out of these meditations, I could not stop crying tears of joy and relief.

Out of these experiences came the planting of the seeds for this book. The more I moved into the subject, the more the message about taking life on its own merit became a pulsating, living force within me. While writing this book, I learned from our Rainmaker, life *was* truly meant to be easy.

Reflections from readers of *Thick Face Black Heart* and *The Asian Mind Game*

Thick Face Black Heart is the best book I've ever read, second only to the Bible as being the greatest work on success principles. Most books on the subject of success are written about actions that have worked for people in their respective circumstances. Your book goes further than the actions themselves and explores the motives and the inner struggles we must face in ourselves.

— W. M., Milledgerville, GA

I would like to tell you that among all the books that I've read, Stephen R. Covey to Silva Mind Control, I sense that I can identify myself with your book, and it really touches me deep inside.

— C.C.C., Malaysia

In order to indicate the perspective and qualifications I bring to the reading of Ms. Chu's books and to the assimilation of her invaluable insights into my teaching and life, let me briefly introduce myself. I am a Professor of Philosophy at California State University at Sacramento, where I have taught for twenty-nine years. (I assign *Thick Face Black Heart* as a required textbook for Philosophy 103: Business and Computer Ethics.) Ethical Identity is perhaps the most critical issue of our time, both as individuals and as a society. Questions about ethical identity are really questions about ethical integrity.

— *D.W.A., Ph.D., Sacramento, CA*

Congratulations for writing such an interesting book—*Thick Face Black Heart*—which I have just read and couldn't stop reading because one learns more and more in each page.

— *G.L.V., Madrid, Spain*

It was with great pleasure that I spent the last eighteen hours reading *Thick Face Black Heart*. Would that it had not ended so soon!

— *K.M., Bondi Junction, NSW, Australia*

Since my stepmother bought me this book, wonderful things have happened. I bought my first house, my business has improved tremendously, my personal finances have also improved. I feel so much better spiritually, mentally, and physically in every way. I must confess that I am a "motivational seminar junkie." I have attended all the seminars that needed to be attended, like Anthony Robbins, Alpha Dynamic Seminars in Australia, various meditation classes. I even went to ashrams in India. Nothing really good happened until your book came along. Your book was all I ever needed. I am quite successful in my field. I am a composer/producer. I had a premiere in Carnegie Hall, New York City (the goal of every musician), with nice write-ups in major media like the *New York Times*. Success in the best revenge for me.

— *E.P., Boston*

You have truly created a classic work of literature in the field of self-development. Over the past five years, I have read more than twenty-five books written to assist people in developing their potential. From Anthony Robbins to Harvey Mackay to Wayne Dyer to Dr. Joseph Murphy—I have read them all, and more. While all of these works helped me to learn key lessons about life and about myself, I want you to know that your book provided me with a fresh viewpoint that has enabled me to get closer to my goal of "pulling it all together."

— *J.A.M., Elmhurst, IL*

I purchased a copy of your book *Thick Face Black Heart* yesterday. What an astounding piece of writing! I am a Native American who has learned to exist and survive in the dominant society. Your book will be very helpful for me to not only exist but succeed.

— *B.A., Eureka, CA*

I am very lucky to have been given a copy of your book *Thick Face Black Heart* by a Malaysian friend. My friend spoke highly of the book and was sure it would benefit a woman like me. He was right.

— *B.G., Manila, Philippines*

Thank you for *Thick Face Black Heart*, as well as for *The Asian Mind Game*. They have become prescribed reading for my MBA class on Leadership and Problem Solving at the Monash Mt. Eliza Business School, Monash University in Melbourne.

— *J.M., Victoria, Australia*

I shared your book with our Taipei-based Price Waterhouse consultants, who recognized it immediately and confirmed its status as the current bestseller in Taiwan.

— *P.J.H., Phoenix, AZ*

I cannot begin to tell you how inspired I was, right from the beginning pages and throughout the book. I have read many books that were described as motivational self-help works. They were beneficial, but I found myself falling back into my old habits shortly after finishing those books. Your book was different. Your exploration into topics such as the attributes of work was particularly compelling. There is rarely a day when I don't reflect back to some section of your book, and occasionally reread it. I have purchased a second copy, since I loaned out my first and found I needed to refer to it.

— *G.J.J., Silver Springs, MD*

I wept when I read your passage about being overwhelmed by a multitude of enemies within yourself.

— *J.A.L., Los Angeles, CA*

It is a fantastic book. I have learned so much from this book about ways to live my personal and business life better. I have been studying Western philosophy for successful living from people such as Tony Robbins, Dennis Waitley, Brian Tracy, Robert Allen, Wayne Dyer, Jim Rohn, etc., and now I study Asian, especially Chinese, philosophy for success in personal and business life.

— *L.L., Surrey, B.C., Canada*

I got your book from the library in a women's prison. This book is so rewarding. I feel like you are a messenger from the Heavens, and I have been graced with wisdom that a lifetime couldn't unfold. Ms. Chu, I just want to make a difference.

Being in prison, I'm surrounded by ignorance that is somehow helping me grow. Your book is such a blessing, and I would like to buy one when I get home. Will you please send me your newsletter and reply to my letter. What is it worth to me? You name it.

— *D.K.L., Stockton, CA*

The *Thick Face Black Heart* seminar held in San Francisco was fabulous from both a business perspective and a personal one.

— *M.L.G., Lowell, MA*

I wanted to let you know I enjoyed your book very much! It is one of the best books I have read, and I can see how it could well become the Think and Grow Rich for the '90s.

— *J.W., Cupertino, CA*

It's a very timely work. I am starting the second reading now. It definitely hit the nail on the head for me!

— *S.J., Antioch, TN*

One of the things that I appreciated about you when we first met was your respect for God and your understanding that universal principles do in fact govern the affairs of human life just as they govern the physical universe.

— *D.H., Hong Kong*

"Somewhere in a meadow, a beautiful flower blooms. It will never appear in the same spot again." Thank you for writing *Thick Face Black Heart*.

— *L.J.D.M., Riyadh, Saudi Arabia*

I just bought your book yesterday evening and finished it today.

— *L.L.Y., Singapore*

I'm a U.S. Marine officer, and I experiment, compare, and apply your intriguing concepts in my daily life.

— *L.G.L., USMC, Japan*

I really enjoy and get a lot of advantage from reading your book *Thick Face Black Heart*.

— *L.S., Jakarta, Indonesia*

I have recommended and purchased your book for a lot of my friends, co-workers, interns, assistants, family, etc. I have even started a *Thick Face Black Heart* focus group to discuss the book.

—*J.A., New York City*

Your book *Thick Face Black Heart* has been an inspiration.

— *W.C.S., Sunninghill, South Africa*

I have read your wonderful, insightful book *Thick Face Black Heart*, and I must tell you that it is slowly working through my system (a.k.a. bringing about a paradigm shift). However, the most important ripple effect of this book will be to appease those morally minded individuals (who think shrewdness is evil) to now proceed firing on all cylinders as they come to realize after reading your book that they are not breaking any Divine code.

— *F.F., Dubai, United Arab Emirates*

I love *Thick Face Black Heart* and have recommended it to at least fifty people. It is my personal manual.

— *D.G., Toronto, Ontario, Canada*

Thank you for the inspirational passages extracted from your excellent book *Thick Face Black Heart*. We can only draw strength and guidance from our inner selves through the outward practice of self-gratification!! Ha, ha, does that sound like a bestseller, or what? Your book was immediately sold out within a few days upon reaching the bookstores in Malaysia.

—*J.W.F.C., Petaling Jaya, Malaysia*

I congratulate you for an excellent book bearing ancient pearls of wisdom and inspiration for the modern world.

— *C.H.L., Victoria, Australia*

Please accept my congratulations upon the accomplishment of such a distinctive and enlightening work as *Thick Face Black Heart*. You have successfully introduced the inner-connectedness of man and his relationship to his world.

— *M.T., Englewood, NJ*

I am writing this letter to thank you personally for your book *Thick Face Black Heart*. This book has changed my life. It has given me an outline and plan for making my dreams and hopes a reality. I find myself using your book daily in making decisions or in forming points-of-view in my life.

— *R.F., El Toro, CA*

Thick Face Black Heart is a book I'd like to read again, so I am ordering a copy for my library as well as one for my brother, who I think would benefit from it.

—*J.S., Hurleyville, NY*

One word I would use to describe your *Thick Face Black Heart* is "AWESOME."

— *E.C.F., Newport Beach, CA*

Your book struck a chord for me, mainly because over the last year or so I have been engaged in personal soul-searching. What I found particularly interesting was the way you integrated in your heart and life both Western and Eastern philosophies and the focus on the spiritual.

— *R.K., San Jose, CA.*

Your emotional honesty is extraordinary because you express yourself so openly in your writing.

— *R.L.S.C., Portland, OR*

Abraham Lincoln is my great-great-uncle. I have read your book *The Asian Mind Game.* After reading your latest book, *Thick Face Black Heart*, I was inspired to write and express my praise.

— *J.P.S., Phoenix, AZ*

I purchased your book *Thick Face Black Heart* at a time when I was very low. I was feeling quite depressed, as things in my life seemed to be at a standstill. Your words have inspired me and renewed my vigor. Without a doubt, I have found this book to be the most inspirational I have ever read. And I am now ready to tackle any problems that life or business can throw at me.

— *D.H., Brisbane, Australia*

Thank you. You don't know me, but you know how I think. Why thank you? Before, I was unknown to myself. Today I know myself better. *Thick Face Black Heart* really helps me in the battle for life.

— *S.G., Japan*

I especially appreciate your emphasis on reconnecting with the actively interested Creator and your skepticism of the superficial "positive thinking" that is normally promoted in self-help literature. The book was substantial, warmly written, and, best of all, unpredictable!

— *P.F.R., Guangzhou, China*

I am taking the liberty to write to you after reading two of your books, *The Asian Mind Game* and *Thick Face Black Heart*, which I found most extraordinarily interesting and well-written. Enclosed you will find a Koala (a stuffed doll), as I understand that you have a soft spot for that Australian animal.

— *P.K.E., Ringsted, Denmark*

Thick Face Black Heart is giving me some missing pieces that I have been looking for, for ten years. Many questions about myself have come to a conclusion.

— *S.W.K., West Palm Beach, FL*

Reading *Thick Face Black Heart* hasn't changed my life, but it has improved my attitude about a great many things. I'm grateful to you for writing it.

— *B.S., Togiak, AL*

This book has changed my life!

— *J.B., Brisbane, Queensland, Australia*

I am writing to tell you of an incredible man, one who has taught this old Chinese much about many things. His name is Steve Hill, and before I return home I wanted to speak of him. He gives all credit to you for his ability to get people to think of others, not just themselves. He gave me a copy of your book *Thick Face Black Heart*, and I feel all can benefit from your teaching. I think it is very good of you to share this wisdom. People like Mr. Hill are proof that the information works. That is all. Through this book, you can have an impact on so many.

— *K.Y., China*

Dear Reader:

If you wish to be on Chin-Ning Chu's mailing list to receive more information on other products or seminars by Chin-Ning, please mail or fax the following information:

Name:_____

Company: _____

Title: _____

Address: _____

_____

State: _____ Postal code: _____

Country: _____

Telephone: _____ Fax: _____

e-mail address: _____

Please contact me regarding having Chin-Ning as the keynote speaker for my company or association's function.

You may contact us at:

Strategic Learning Institute
PO Box 2986
Antioch, CA 94531
Tel: (510) 777-1888; Fax: (510) 777-1238
e-mail address: cnc@strategic.org